ROBERT BURNS
and his world

DAVID DAICHES

ROBERT BURNS
and his world

with 120 illustrations

THAMES AND HUDSON

Frontispiece. Robert Burns, from a
sketch by Alexander Nasmyth,
c. 1787. The oil painting reproduced
here was made from the sketch in
1828 for Lockhart's *Life of Burns*.

© *1971 David Daiches*
Reprinted 1978
*Originally published in the United
States of America in 1972 by The
Viking Press, Inc.*

*Library of Congress Catalog card
number: 77–92264*

Printed in Great Britain

Map of Ayrshire, *c.* 1756. 'The face of the country . . . appeared rough and dark, consisting greatly of heath, moss, patches of straggling wood and rudely cultivated grounds.' (Rev. John Mitchell, *Memories of Ayrshire about 1780*)

It was probably on his twenty-eighth birthday that Robert Burns looked back to his first birthday, 25 January 1759, and celebrated it (as it has been celebrated so often since) with a song:

> *There was a lad was born in Kyle,*
> *But what na day o' what na style*
> *I doubt it's hardly worth the while*
> *To be sae nice wi' Robin.*

which

Kyle is the district of Ayrshire between the rivers Irvine and Doon, the latter of which Burns was to make famous in another song. The village of Alloway, two and a half miles south of Ayr and now a suburb of that town, lies by the Doon, and

5

Burns's cottage, Alloway. The 'auld clay biggin' built by Burns's father with his own hands. Now a Burns museum.

Burns was born there in a clay cottage which his father had built with his own hands:

> Our monarch's hindmost year but ane
> Was five-and-twenty days begun,
> 'Twas then a blast o' Janwar' Win'   January wind
> Blew hansel in on Robin.   new-year gift

The story went that when the baby was nine or ten days old a gale blew down part of the cottage and he had to be carried through the storm to a neighbour's house where he remained until repairs were effected. It was a stormy beginning to a stormy life.

'I have not the most distant pretensions to what the pye-coated guardians of escutcheons call, A Gentleman', Burns wrote in August 1787 in a famous auto-biographical letter to Dr John Moore. His father William Burnes (as he spelt his name) had come to Ayrshire from Kincardineshire, on the other side of Scotland further north, via Edinburgh, where he had worked as a gardener helping to lay out the park now known as The Meadows. He had left his native county with reluc-tance, apparently because his farming schemes had been wrecked by the aftermath of the Jacobite Rebellion of 1745. William Burnes's father had been a tenant of the Earl Marischal, and Robert liked to think that his grandfather had joined that Jacobite in the 1715 rebellion. William Burnes may have come under suspicion after the '45, though it is hard to imagine this stern though not unkindly Presbyterian as sympathetic to the Jacobite cause. There was certainly no suspicion of Jacobitism in the family of his bride Agnes Broun, who were Ayrshire tenant farmers in the Cove-nanting tradition. Married and anxious to improve his position, William Burnes

Agnes Broun (1732–1820). Burns's sister, Mrs Begg, described her mother as 'rather under the average height; inclined to plumpness, but neat, shapely, and full of energy; having a beautiful pink-and-white complexion, a fine square forehead, pale red hair, but dark eyebrows, and dark eyes often ablaze with a temper difficult to control.'

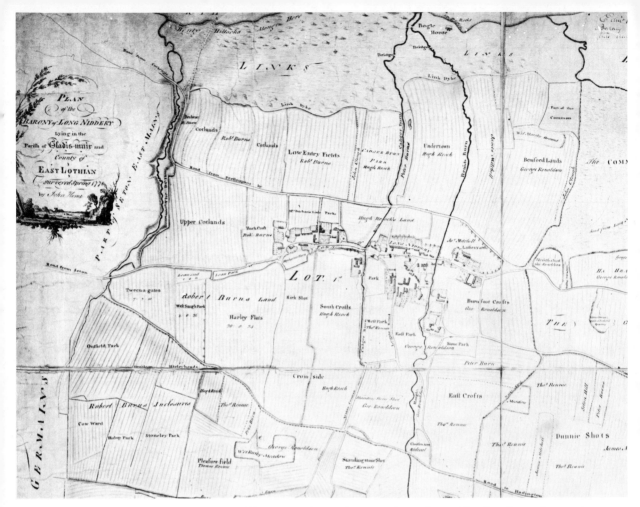

The estate of Longniddry, East Lothian. These two plans, of 1778 (above) and 1792 (opposite), illustrate very clearly the process of consolidation and enlargement of holdings which went on throughout Lowland Scotland during Burns's lifetime.

gave up the job of head gardener on the estate of one Dr Fergusson, a wealthy retired medical practitioner, and in 1765 leased the farm of Mount Oliphant, a few miles east of Alloway – seventy acres of ill-drained ground at the uneconomic rent of forty pounds a year for the first six years and forty-five pounds a year for the next six. In 1777 he moved to the 130-acre farm of Lochlie, ten miles to the north-east, for which he paid an even more inflated rent of one pound per acre per year. It proved a ruinous bargain, and the struggle to make something of it caused his bankruptcy and premature death early in 1784.

William Burnes was a man of character and intelligence; it was not his fault that he failed as a farmer. This was a period of rapid transition in Scottish farming. In the course of the eighteenth century the old system of cultivating land in ridges, with,

8

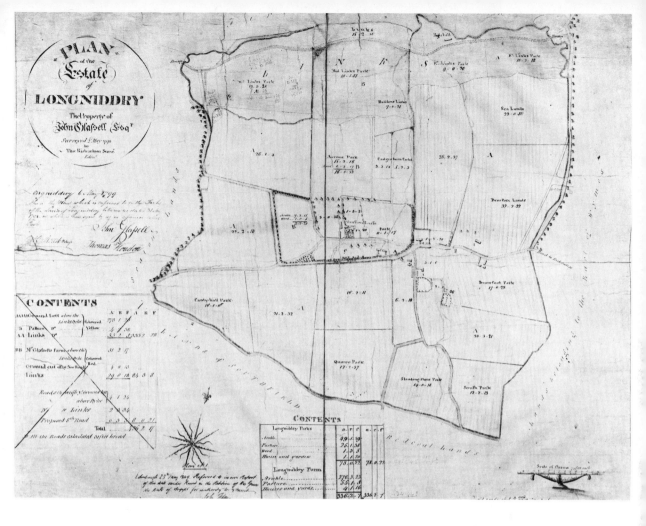

in the words of a late eighteenth-century parish minister, 'the ridges of arable land [belonging] alternately to different tenants, a most incommodious and absurd arrangement', was giving way to the enclosure of previously open farmland with the consolidation and enlargement of holdings, improved soil drainage, and other forms of modernization. In William Burnes's time the rise of farm rents in the anticipation of improvement had far outstripped actual improvements. And arable farming in Ayrshire had special disadvantages. The overseer of Sir John Whitefoord's Ballochmyle estate wrote in 1778: 'As the climate is rainy, and the land clay, and having early frosts in autumn, the practice of corn husbandry is attended with many difficulties, which would require all the industry and attention of the most active to surmount.'

9

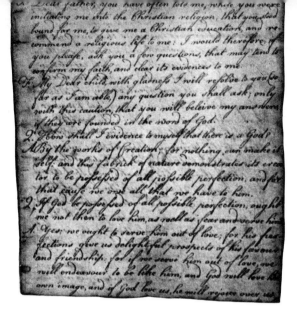

Manuscript copy by John Murdoch of 'A Manual of Religious Belief in a Dialogue between Father and Son', believed to have been written by William Burnes.

Early life Robert was six years old when his father exchanged his position of gardener for that of tenant farmer. Had he not done so, wrote Robert in 1787, 'I must have marched off to be one of the little underlings about a farm house; but it was his dearest wish and prayer to keep his children under his own eye till they could discern between good and evil'. Like so many Scottish peasants, William Burnes was a reading and thinking man with a fondness for philosophical and theological discourse, and he wished to bring up his children to be both educated and God fearing. As late as 1811, the writer of the *Agricultural Report* on Ayrshire observed that 'an extensive acquaintance with the mysterious, abstruse and disputed points of systematic divinity, was the species of knowledge farmers generally sought after, and to which the greatest fame was attached.' The womenfolk as a rule did not share this interest. Agnes Burnes was barely literate, though skilled in domestic duties appropriate to a farm and possessed of a good voice and a fine store of songs that were to play an important part in Robert's education as a poet. Even more important was the part played by an illiterate female relative who helped in the farmhouse: 'In my infant and boyish days,' wrote Burns to Dr Moore, 'I owed much to an old Maid of my Mother's, remarkable for her ignorance, credulity and superstition. – She had, I suppose, the largest collection in the county of tales and songs concerning devils, ghosts, fairies, brownies, witches, warlocks, spunkies, kelpies, elf candles, dead lights, wraiths, apparitions, cantraips, giants, inchanted towers, dragons and other trumpery. This cultivated the latent seeds of Poesy.'

When Robert was in his sixth year and the family was still at Alloway, he was sent to a school at Alloway Miln, about a mile away. A few months later, however, the teacher there was appointed master of the Ayr workhouse and William Burnes then joined with some other farming families in the neighbourhood to hire jointly a young man called John Murdoch to teach their children. In a letter written in 1799 Murdoch gave an account of his teaching:

'. . . In the month of May [1765] I was engaged by Mr Burnes, and four of his neighbours, to teach, and accordingly began to teach the little school at Alloway, which was situated a few yards from the argillaceous fabric above/mentioned. [This was the clay cottage in which the Burnes family lived. One of Murdoch's favourite teaching devices was to encourage his pupils to produce lists of synonyms, the more pretentious the better.] My five employers undertook to board me by turns, and to make up a certain salary at the end of the year, provided my quarterly payments from the different pupils did not amount to that sum.

'My pupil Robert Burns, was then between six and seven years of age; his pre/ceptor [i.e., Murdoch himself], about eighteen. Robert and his younger brother Gilbert, had been grounded a little in English, before they were put under my care. They both made a rapid progress in reading; and a tolerable progress in writing. In reading, dividing words into syllables by rule, spelling without book, parsing sentences, &c. Robert and Gilbert were generally at the upper end of the class, even when ranged with boys by far their seniors. The books most commonly used in the school were, the *Spelling Book*, the *New Testament*, the *Bible, Mason's* [actually, *Masson's*] *Collection of Prose and Verse*, and *Fisher's English Grammar*. . . . As soon as they were capable of it, I taught them to turn verse into its natural prose order; sometimes to substitute synonimous expressions for poetical words, and to supply all the ellipses. These, you know, are the means of knowing that the pupil under/stands his author. These are excellent helps to the arrangement of words in sen/tences, as well as to a variety of expressions.'

When it is realized that Masson's *Collection* contained passages from Shakespeare, Milton and Dryden as well as from eighteenth/century English poets including Thomson, Gray and Shenstone and prose selections from Addison and from Mrs Elizabeth Rowe's *Letters Moral and Entertaining*, it will be appreciated that little Robert got a pretty good grounding in English literature. He got no formal instruc/tion in Scottish literature; this, as far as the folk tradition went, he picked up him/self from the songs and stories he heard all around him, while the more formal aspects of older Scottish literature he either learned from debased chapbook ver/sions (such as the modernized version of the fifteenth/century poem *Wallace*, which he borrowed from Candlish the blacksmith and which fired him with a patriotic Scottish zeal that never left him) or read for himself after he had developed his own poetic ambitions and was consciously seeking to improve his knowledge of Scottish poetry.

It is important to realize that Burns learned as a small boy to write accurate and somewhat literary standard English. At the same time, his normal speech in the

Ayr, *c.* 1800.

countryside was Ayrshire Scots, though he was perfectly capable of speaking an elegant formal English when the occasion called for it. A contemporary who heard both Robert Burns and David Hume speak in Edinburgh (not at the same time, for Hume died in 1776, more than ten years before Burns first visited the Scottish capital) reported that Hume had a stronger Scottish accent than Burns.

Murdoch gave up teaching Burns and his young contemporaries after nearly two and a half years, but in 1772 he obtained a teaching position at Ayr and in 1773 Robert was sent to board with him there, in Murdoch's words, 'for the purpose of revising his English grammar, &c. that he might be better qualified to instruct his brothers and sisters at home'. Murdoch instructed him assiduously and, Burns's English grammar now being perfect, decided to ground him in French. 'Now there was little else to be heard but the declensions of nouns, the conjugation of verbs, &c. When walking together, and even at meals, I was constantly telling him the names of different objects, as they presented themselves, in French; so that he was hourly laying in a stock of words, and sometimes little phrases. In short, he took such pleasure in learning, and I in teaching, that it was difficult to say which of the two was most zealous in the business; and about the end of the second week of our study of the French, we began to read a little of the *Adventures of Telemachus*, in Fénelon's own words.' Burns went on to acquire a reasonable reading knowledge of the language, but one wonders how someone who was later to rhyme *respectueuse* with 'Susie' pronounced it.

But Robert, as Murdoch characteristically put it, 'was summoned to relinquish the pleasing scenes that surrounded the grotto of Calypso, and, armed with a sickle, to seek glory by signalizing himself in the fields of Ceres'. He had to help on the farm, and it was strenuous work. Life at Mount Oliphant was hard. Robert's brother Gilbert later recalled it:

'Nothing could be more retired than our general manner of living. . . . My father *Life on the farm* was for some time almost the only companion we had. He conversed familiarly on all subjects with us as if we had been men, and was at great pains while we accompanied him in the labours of the farm, to lead the conversation to such subjects as might tend to encrease our knowledge, or confirm us in virtuous habits. He borrowed *Salmon's Geographical Grammar* for us, and endeavoured to make us acquainted with the situation and history of the different countries in the world; while from a book-society in Ayr, he procured for us the reading of *Derham's Physico and Astro-theology*, and *Ray's Wisdom of God in the Creation* [these were three popular textbooks of science which presented scientific facts as evidence of the existence of an ingenious and benevolent Creator], to give us some idea of astronomy and natural history. Robert read all these books with an avidity and industry scarcely to be equalled. My father had been a subscriber to *Stackhouse's History of the Bible* [a lively re-telling of biblical narrative with historical and textual notes] . . . from this Robert collected a competent knowledge of ancient history. . . .'

An uncle bought 'a collection of letters by the Wits of Queen Anne's reign' in mistake for something else, and Robert pounced on it. 'It inspired him,' said Gilbert, 'with a strong desire to excel in letter-writing, while it furnished him with models by some of the first writers in our language.' Shortly before his stay with Murdoch in Ayr, Robert was sent for a short period to the parish school of Dalrymple to improve his handwriting. About the same time 'a bookish acquaintance' of his father's introduced him to Richardson's *Pamela*, and he went on to read Fielding and Smollett and the historical works of David Hume and William Robertson. He devoured everything he could lay hands on. The gardener of a neighbouring landowner lent him a history of James I and Charles I. Murdoch sent him the works of Pope and some other volumes of English poetry. On his return to the farm from Ayr, a friend of Murdoch's, hearing of his progress with French, offered to help him with Latin, and on his advice Robert bought a Latin grammar with which he made intermittent progress. But he never acquired more than the merest smattering of the language.

It must have required enormous will power to study at Mount Oliphant. Again, Gilbert tells the story:

'We lived very sparingly. For several years butcher's meat was a stranger in the house, while all the members of the family exerted themselves to the utmost of their strength, and rather beyond it, in the labours of the farm. My brother at the age of

Farming scene. Pen drawing by the Scottish artist, William Allan.

thirteen assisted in threshing the crop of corn, and at fifteen was the principal labourer on the farm, for we had no hired servant, male or female. The anguish of mind we felt at our tender years, under these straits and difficulties, was very great. To think of our father growing old (for he was now above fifty) broken down with the long continued fatigues of his life, with a wife and five other children, and in a declining state of circumstances, these reflections produced in my brother's mind and mine sensations of the deepest distress. I doubt not but the hard labour and sorrow of this period of his life, was in a great measure the cause of that depression of spirits with which Robert was so often afflicted through his whole life afterwards. At this time he was almost constantly afflicted in the evenings with a dull headache, which at a future period of his life, was exchanged for a palpitation of the heart, and a threatening of fainting and suffocation in his bed, in the night time.'

In fact, a combination of excessive physical labour and insufficiently nutritious food in youth produced in Robert the first symptoms of that rheumatic heart disease which was eventually to cause his death. Robert told Dr Moore of the hard years:

'My father's generous Master died; the farm proved a ruinous bargain; and, to clench the curse, we fell into the hands of a Factor who sat for the picture I have drawn of one in my Tale of two dogs. – My father was advanced in life when he married; I was the eldest of seven children; and he, worn out by early hardship, was unfit for labour. . . . There was a freedom in his lease in two years more, and to weather these two years we retrenched expences. – We lived very poorly; I was a dextrous Ploughman for my years; and the next eldest to me was a brother, who

14

could drive the plough very well and help me to thrash. – A Novel-Writer might perhaps have viewed these scenes with some satisfaction, but so did not I: my indignation yet boils at the recollection of the scoundrel tyrant's insolent, threatening epistles, which used to set us all in tears.

'This kind of life, the chearless gloom of a hermit with the unceasing moil of a galley-slave, brought me to my sixteenth year; a little before which period I first committed the sin of RHYME. . . .'

The factor, or landlord's agent, who so aroused Burns's indignation appears, as he says, in *The Twa Dogs*, written probably late in 1785:

> *I've notic'd, on our Laird's court-day,*
> *An' mony a time my heart's been wae,*
> *Poor tenant-bodies, scant o' cash,*
> *How they maun thole a factor's snash;*   must bear   abuse
> *He'll stamp an' threaten, curse an' swear,*
> *He'll apprehend them, poind their gear,*   distrain their goods
> *While they maun stand, wi' aspect humble,*
> *An' hear it a', an' fear an' tremble!*

In the midst of these troubles, William Burnes was still thinking of his children's education. In the summer of 1775 Robert was sent south-west to the town of Kirkoswald, some two miles from the coast, to 'a noted school, to learn Mensuration, Surveying, Dialling, &c. in which I made a pretty good progress'. But, as he told Dr Moore, he made greater progress in his knowledge of mankind:

'The contraband trade was at the time very successful; scenes of swaggering riot and roaring dissipation were as yet new to me; and I was no enemy to social life. –

Brawl outside an alehouse. Detail of a painting by Alexander Carse.

Here, though I learned to look unconcernedly on a large tavern-bill, and mix without fear in a drunken squabble, yet I went on with a high hand in my Geo-metry; till the sun entered Virgo, a month which is always a carnival in my bosom, a charming Fillette [her name was Peggy Thompson, 'once fondly lov'd, and still remember'd dear', as he later wrote in inscribing a copy of his first volume of poems to her; she married a friend of his] who lived next door to the school overset my Trigonomertry [*sic*], and set me off in a tangent from the sphere of my studies. – I struggled on with my Sines and Co-sines for a few days more; but stepping out to the garden one charming noon, to take the sun's altitude, I met with my Angel,

> – *"Like Proserpine gathering flowers,*
> *Herself a fairer flower"* –

It was vain to think of doing any more good at school. – The remaining week I staid, I did nothing but craze the faculties of my soul about her, or steal out to meet with her; and the two last nights of my stay in the country, had sleep been a mortal sin, I was innocent. –

'I returned home very considerably improved. – My reading was enlarged with the very important addition of Thomson's and Shenstone's works; I had seen mankind in a new phasis; and I engaged several of my schoolfellows to keep up a literary correspondence with me. . . .'

First love songs So life was not always 'the chearless gloom of a hermit with the unceasing moil of a galley-slave'. Burns was in fact very much up and down, alternating periods of light-hearted gaiety with moods of profound depression. He attended a country dancing school 'to give my manners a brush' in spite of his father's forbidding it. His defiance of his father caused a breach which he lived to regret. Since the autumn of 1773, when he had been smitten by the charms of a girl with whom he had been working at harvest, he had been falling in love regularly, relishing that 'delicious Passion, which in spite of acid Disappointment, gin-horse Prudence and book-worm Philosophy, I hold to be the first of human joys, our dearest pleasure here below.' Love inspired him to write love songs. 'I was not so presumtive as to imagine that I could make verses like printed ones, composed by men who had Greek and Latin; but my girl sung a song which was said to be composed by a small country laird's son, on one of his father's maids, with whom he was in love; and I saw no reason why I might not rhyme as well as he'. So, when not quite sixteen, he wrote his first love poem, to Nelly Kirkpatrick, daughter of a farmer at Dalrymple, set to the tune (which we do not know) 'I am a man unmarried'. When he began his Commonplace Book in April 1783 he inscribed this song, with the observation: 'For my own part I never had the least thought or inclination of turning Poet till I got once heartily in Love, and then Rhyme & Song were, in a manner, the spontaneous language of my heart.' In recalling the incident in his

16

Highland dancing was immensely popular in the latter half of the eighteenth century and there were many collections of dance tunes. To some of these tunes, slowed down in tempo, Burns wrote songs.

The Braes of Athole.

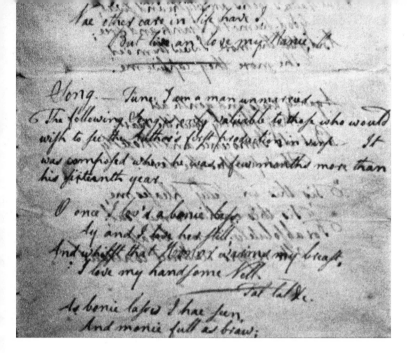

O once I lov'd a bonie lass. Entered in Burns's Commonplace Book in April 1783.

letter to Dr Moore, he concluded: 'Thus with me began Love and Poesy.' But Love and Poesy were only two of the associated factors. Music was a third: he had to have a tune running through his head before he could write a love song. And Ambition or Emulation was a fourth. 'I had felt early some stirrings of Ambition', he told Dr Moore, but did not know how or where to direct them. From a very early age Burns had resented his social inferiority. He was thrown together in childhood (as was common in the Scottish countryside) with the children of landowners who had considerable prospects, and he bitterly resented that when they grew up they would move in higher spheres and look down on him. 'I formed many connections with other Youngkers who possessed superiour advantages; the youngling Actors who were busy with the rehearsal of PARTS in which they were shortly to appear on that STAGE where, Alas! I was destined to drudge behind the SCENES.' Burns never lost his belief that rank had nothing to do with worth, that it was intolerable for a man of inferior parts to give himself airs merely because he had rank or property – that, in short, 'a man's a man for a' that'.

The family moved to Lochlie at Whitsun 1777, and again the story can be told in Burns's words to Dr Moore:

'For four years we lived comfortably here; but a lawsuit between him and his Landlord commencing, after three years tossing and whirling in the vortex of Litigation, my father was just saved from absorption in a jail by phthisical consumption, which after two years promises, kindly stept in and snatch'd him away – "To where the wicked cease from troubling, and where the weary be at rest".'

18

The first four years at Lochlie were probably the happiest ever spent by the Burns family as a whole. Robert made friends in the nearby villages of Tarbolton and Mauchline, and with some of these he founded the Tarbolton Bachelors' Club in November 1780. This was a debating society which met every fourth Monday evening to discuss such topics as: 'Suppose a young man, bred a farmer, but without any fortune, has it in his power to marry either of two women, the one a girl of large fortune, but neither handsome in person, nor agreeable in conversation, but who can manage the household affairs of a farm well enough; the other of them a girl every way agreeable, in person, conversation, and behaviour, but without any fortune: which of them shall he choose?' (This was the topic discussed at the first meeting, when Burns was chosen president for the night and doubtless suggested the subject.) Burns for the first time found an audience, which gave him confidence and encouraged the development of his talents. None of the other members had his intelligence or his vivid personality, but they acted as a sounding-board and stimulated his wit and his pride. They are remembered now because

Lochlie Farm.

Tarbolton. '. . . The rude aspect of nature has here, long since, given place to the beauties and the wealth of industrious cultivation.' (*Statistical Account of Scotland*, 1798)

The town of Mauchline.

Burns was to write verse epistles to them. David Sillar, himself a versifier, John Rankine, a coarse-mouthed but lively and humorous farmer, and others helped to define and encourage Burns's ambition. Sillar later remembered the young Burns:

'Mr Robert Burns was sometime in the parish of Tarbolton prior to my acquaintance with him. His social disposition easily procured him acquaintance; but a certain satirical seasoning, with which he and all poetical geniuses are in some degree influenced, while it set the rustic circle in a roar, was not unaccompanied by its kindred attendant – suspicious fear. I recollect hearing his neighbours observe he had a great deal to say for himself, and that they suspected his *principles*. He wore the only tied hair in the parish; and in the church, his plaid, which was of a particular colour, I think *fillemot*, he wrapped in a peculiar manner around his shoulders. . . .'

Burns himself described his life at this time to Dr Moore in this way:

'My life flowed on much in the same tenor till my twenty third year. – Vive l'amour et vive la bagatelle, were my sole principles of action. – The addition of two more Authors to my library gave me great pleasure; Sterne and McKenzie [Henry Mackenzie, author of the popular sentimental novel *The Man of Feeling*]. – Tristram Shandy and the Man of Feeling were my bosom favourites. – Poesy was still a darling walk for my mind, but 'twas only the humour of the hour. – I had usually half a dozen or more pieces on hand; I took up one or other as it suited the momentary tone of the mind, and dismissed it as bordering on fatigue. – My Passions when once they were lighted up, raged like so many devils, till they got vent in rhyme; and then conning over my verses, like a spell, soothed all into quiet.'

A bit of an exhibitionist, desperately anxious to improve himself by reading and corresponding, suspect by the respectable for his outspokenness, subject to moods of exaltation and depression, writing poetry as a therapy – the picture of Burns as he entered his twenties is clear enough. In 1780 or 1781 he fell in love with Alison Begbie, daughter of a small farmer and at the time working as a servant in a nearby house, and wrote her love letters in a curiously stilted English (they are among the earliest of Burns's letters that survive). He appears to have proposed marriage to her and to have been rejected. His last letter to her talks of the shock of her reply to a letter of his and continues: 'It would be weak and unmanly to say that without you I can never be happy; but sure I am, that sharing life with you, would have given it a relish, that, wanting you, I can never taste.' Burns was often employed to write love letters for his less articulate friends, and it is possible that what we have here are letters written for another, but there is reason for believing the tradition that associates them with Burns's third love affair and his most important so far.

But of course the farm claimed most of Robert's attention. He and his brother Gilbert were anxious to improve conditions on the farm, and they rented from their father about three acres for the cultivation of flax. Earlier in the century John Cockburn of Ormiston, East Lothian, had established a linen industry in his own neighbourhood and brought in experts from Ireland and Holland to teach his tenants how to prepare flax. In 1726 the Convention of Royal Burghs had pressed for legislation to encourage the growing of flax and bleaching of linen in Scotland. Lint mills were set up throughout the country and improved heckles (flax combs) were imported from Holland and England. The British Linen Company (a purely Scottish company, in spite of its name) was founded in 1746 to provide the growing number of linen manufacturers with finance. As the century advanced, it looked more and more as though flax, which earlier had been grown in Scotland in small quantities for household needs only, was to become an important crop. True, Sir John Whitefoord's overseer at Ballochmyle reported in 1778 that he had 'tried flax, but think it scourges the land, and deprives the cattle of fodder, and, upon the whole, is not profitable here [in Ayrshire].' But the Burns brothers wanted to give it a trial and indeed their father had some thought of turning over the whole farm to flax. Spurred by these ideas, in the summer of 1781 Robert went to Irvine, a flourishing seaport north of Ayr and a centre of the flax-dressing industry, to learn how to dress flax. Irvine was the biggest and busiest town Burns had yet seen. It contained sailors and smugglers ('the young men, in general, are sailors, or go abroad to the West Indies and America as storekeepers and planters', wrote the

Trade Card for the Linen Hall, Edinburgh, which was established in 1766. It did not prove a success since manufacturers preferred to deal directly with customers, and was closed in 1790.

Flax-dressing scene in Ireland, which was Scotland's chief competitor in linen manufacture in the latter half of the eighteenth century. Scottish flax-dressers used the same method.

parish minister a decade later), prosperous merchants, many weavers, and exporters of carpets and of coal. 'The people, in general,' the minister reported, 'are in easy circumstances; many of them are wealthy, and all of them remarkably hospitable. They are happy in each other's society, and entertain frequently and well.' For Burns, Irvine proved an exciting and dangerous town.

He arrived there in a vulnerable state of mind. Mortified by his rejection by Alison Begbie, troubled by his father's increasing ill-health and worsening economic situation, attacked intermittently by what he called 'that most dreadful distemper, a Hypochondria, or confirmed Melancholy', he tried to overcome his gloom by plunging into such social delights as the town afforded. He developed a warm friendship with Richard Brown, an educated young sailor with a romantic history whose 'courage, independence, Magnanimity, and every noble, manly virtue', as he put it to Dr Moore, he admired and sought to imitate. He also admired Brown's knowledge of the world and his way with women: it seems to have been Brown who first broke down Burns's inhibition against fornication – his love affairs hitherto had been innocent. But most important of all, Brown encouraged Burns to take himself seriously as a poet. 'Do you recollect a sunday we spent in Eglinton woods?' he wrote Brown in December 1787, 'you told me on my repeating some verses to you, that you wondered I could resist the temptation of sending verses of such merit to a magazine: 'twas actually this that gave me an idea of my own

23

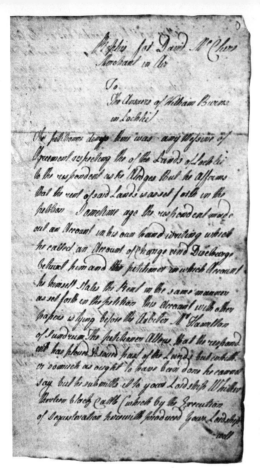

First page of the service copy petition by David M'Lure, landlord of Lochlie, against William Burnes. In leasing the farm to the latter, he failed to make the precise terms clear, and this led to subsequent legislation.

pieces which encouraged me to endeavour at the character of a Poet.' He had almost given up poetry, except for gloomy moralizing pieces written in fits of depression, but Brown's encouragement and the providential discovery of Robert Fergusson's Scots poems (on reading which he 'strung anew [his] wildly-sounding, rustic lyre with emulating vigour') brought new poetic excitement.

Burns's stay in Irvine ended in tragi-comedy. The flax-dresser, with whom he had entered into partnership with a view to learning his trade, turned out to be a scoundrel and a thief. Finally, when he, his partner and his partner's wife were bringing in the new year (1782) with the traditional carousing, carelessness on the part of the partner's wife led to their shop, in which the party was being held, being set on fire and burnt to ashes. Burns was 'left, like a true Poet, not worth sixpence'. He returned to Lochlie in the early spring of 1782, the venture into flax having been a total failure. Things at the farm got steadily worse. William Burnes became involved in a legal dispute over the amount of the rent and the person to whom it was legally payable, and exhausted and impoverished himself in litigation. He died a bankrupt in February 1784.

William Burnes's grave, Alloway Auld Kirk. This is the third gravestone. The original one, erected by the poet, was carried away in chips by visitors eager to have relics of the family. ▶

Robert Burns and Gavin Hamilton at Nanse Tinnock's alehouse, Mauchline. It had a rear door opening directly into the churchyard to enable thirsty sermon-tasters to discuss the sermon over liquid refreshment without loss of time. Nanse Tinnock's must not be confused with Poosie Nancy's, another Mauchline tavern, and the scene of *The Jolly Beggars*.

Silhouette of Robert Burns. Silhouette of Gilbert Burns.

In anticipation of their father's death, Robert and Gilbert had entered into negotiations with Gavin Hamilton, a liberal-minded Mauchline lawyer, to rent from him the farm of Mossgiel, half way between Mauchline and Lochlie, which Hamilton had himself leased from the Earl of Loudon whose factor he was. Because William Burnes had paid his sons wages for their labour on the farm, they were able to get themselves legally recognized as preferred creditors after William's death and thus to save something from the wreck of the family's fortunes. They moved the few miles to Mossgiel in the early spring of 1784. The landlord was helpful. The rent, ninety pounds per annum for 118 acres, was more reasonable than the pound per acre that William had paid at Lochlie. Robert, as he later recalled, 'entered on this farm with a full resolution'. He studied books on agriculture and conscientiously attended markets. But the heavy clay soil of Mossgiel, with much of the top-soil removed by heavy rain and bad farming methods, did not respond.

'The farm of Mossgiel [Gilbert Burns later wrote] lies very high, and mostly on a cold wet bottom. The first four years that we were on the farm were very frosty, and the spring was very late. Our crops in consequence were very unprofitable, and notwithstanding our utmost diligence and economy, we found ourselves obliged to give up our bargain, with the loss of a considerable part of our original stock.'

27

Mossgiel in Burns's time.

Mossgiel Farm, Mauchline. 'When my father's affairs drew near a crisis, Robert and I took the farm of Mossgiel . . . as an asylum for the family in case of the worst.'
(Gilbert Burns)

Interior of the kitchen, Mossgiel.

Mauchline. According to the *Statistical Account of Scotland*, the town had a population of 1000 in 1791.

It was not the brothers' fault. The whole family worked hard and lived frugally. Robert and Gilbert allowed themselves seven pounds per annum each. Indeed, every member of the family received a humble labourer's wage for work on the farm. Throughout the four years Robert never spent more than his meagre annual wage.

If Robert's financial habits, as Gilbert testified, were characterized by 'temperance and frugality', the same cannot be said of his emotional life. He was now head of the household, 'Rab Mossgiel', a figure known in the countryside and neighbouring towns (especially Mauchline, only about a mile away) as an articulate, temperamental, witty, proud (yet at the same time convivial), irreverent and even dangerous character. Though he had admired and loved his father, he could not but feel his death as something of a liberation. Elizabeth Paton, who had been a farm servant in the Burns household, bore his first illegitimate child in May 1785. The mother did not expect marriage; Burns handed the baby girl over to his own complacent mother to rear and welcomed his daughter with a poem in an old Scottish stanza which showed his pleasure at finding himself a father in spite of the irregularity:

little one   *Thou's welcome, Wean! Mischanter fa' me,*   mishaps befall
If thoughts o' thee, or yet thy Mamie,
Shall ever daunton me or awe me,
My bonie lady;
Or if I blush when thou shalt ca' me
Tyta, or Daddie.

In any study of Burns it is impossible to avoid some discussion of his sexual   *Sexual activities*
activities, and there will be more of these to recount. But though Burns's sexual problems proved to be unique, he was far from unique in his country fornications. The simple fact is that such activity was one of the few pleasures available to the Scottish peasantry, and in spite of the thunderings of the Kirk and the ritual of public humiliation it imposed on offenders – sometimes driving the girl to suicide – it remained extremely common throughout Burns's lifetime. Indeed, the Kirk's

A Poet's Welcome to his Love-begotten Daughter, from the Glenriddell ms. An earlier ms. preserves Burns's original title: *The Poet's Welcome to His Bastart Wean.* ▶

A Poet's welcome to his love-begotten daughter: the
first instance that entitled him to the venerable appellation
of, Father.————   MSS v 2 fo 279

Thou's welcome, Wean! Mischanter fa' me,
 If thoughts o' thee, or yet thy Mammie,
Shall ever daunton me or awe me,
                My bonie lady;
Or if I blush when thou shalt ca' me
                ~~Tyta~~, or Daddie.

Tho' now they name me, Fornicator,
 And tease my name in kintra clatter,
The mair they talk, I'm kend the better,
                E'en let them clash!
An auld wife's tongue 's a feckless matter
                To gie ane fash.

Welcome! My bonie, sweet, wee Dochter!
Tho' ye come here a wee unsought for,
And tho' your comin I hae fought for,
                Baith Kirk & Queir;
Yet by my faith, ye're no unwrought for,
                That I shall swear!

Wee image, o' my bonie Betty,
As fatherly I kiss & daut thee,

As dear & near my heart I set thee,
        Wi' as gude will,
As a' the Priests had seen me get thee
        That's out o' h——.——

Sweet fruit o' monie a merry dint,
My funny toil is no a' tint;
Tho' ye come to the warld asklent,
        Which fools may scoff at,
In my last plack your part's be in't
        The better half o't.——

Tho' I should be the waur bestead,
Thou's be as braw & bienly clad,
And thy young years be nicely bred
        Wi' education,
As ony brat o' Wedlock's bed
        In a' thy station.——

For if thou be, what I wad hae thee,
And tak the counsel I shall gie thee,
I'll never rue my trouble wi' thee,
        The cost nor shame o't,
But be a loving Father to thee,
        And brag the name o't.——

rules recognized fornication as a normal fact of life by laying down a procedure by which the erring father, by receiving public rebuke for his fault, was released of any marital obligation and officially recognized as still a bachelor. Burns himself went through this procedure with Jean Armour, with whom he had become very seriously involved in the summer of 1785 and whom, after many vicissitudes, he eventually married. Oddly enough Burns, for all his sexual adventuring, was in a deep sense a family man whose ideal was sitting at the domestic fireside 'wi' weans and wife'. Further, he was wholly outside the Don Juan tradition in his delight at the idea of parenthood and his ability to associate sexual pleasure with joy in children. His poem *O wha my babie-clouts will buy?*, written probably for Jean when she was about to bear his illegitimate child, puts into the girl's mouth both pride in the baby, pride in the father, and anticipation of further sexual pleasure: no other love poet in the language has ever achieved such an audacious combination:

Growth of a poet

> *O wha my babie-clouts will buy?*
> *O wha will tent me when I cry?*   care for
> *Wha will kiss me where I lie?*
> *The ranting dog, the daddie o't. . . .*

But Burns was writing more than love poems. In the religious disputes that so

Lovers in a barn. From a painting by George Morland. '*And I'll kiss thee yet, yet.*'

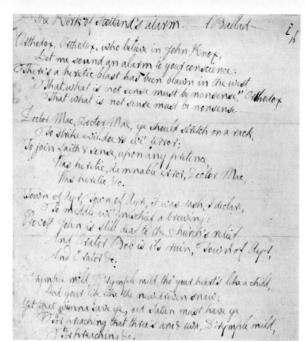

The Kirk of Scotland's Alarm. The occasion of the poem was a complaint lodged by the Presbytery of Ayr against the minister, William M'Gill ('Doctor Mac') in July 1789.

bitterly rent eighteenth- and early nineteenth-century Scotland and which produced so many schisms and disruptions, Burns, like his landlord Gavin Hamilton, was on the side of the liberal-minded moderates, who preferred moral works to Calvinist orthodoxy and strict sabbatarian discipline, and were against the rigidly orthodox with their Calvinistic insistence on original sin, election and predestination. When Scotland had lost its Parliament in 1707 and become no longer an independent country but a part of Great Britain, it had retained its own legal institutions and its own Presbyterian Church. Disputes about the right of lay patrons to appoint ministers led early to internecine disputes in the Church of Scotland, and after 1747 this matter got mixed up with a dispute about public office-holders taking an oath of loyalty to the established religion. By Burns's time generations of divisions and sub-divisions had split essentially into the 'Auld Lichts', the rigid Calvinists, and the more moderate, liberal 'New Lichts'. Burns supported the latter, especially after his friendly landlord had a run-in with 'Daddy' Auld, the minister at Mauchline. He wrote and circulated among his friends some brilliant poetical satires on Auld Licht characters, notably *The Holy Tulzie* [quarrel, brawl], 'a burlesque lamentation on a quarrel between two rev^d Calvinists'; *Holy Willie's Prayer*, a devastating exposure of the hypocrisy that the Calvinist doctrine of election may breed in those who believe themselves one of the elect – an exposure made all the more effective by being put into the mouth of a Calvinist who all unwittingly exposes himself; and *The Holy Fair*, a poem in the Scottish tradition of celebrations of popular revelry in which he uses an old Scottish stanza form he had learned from Fergusson to describe with enormous relish the various goings-on at one of the

33

A sleepy congregation.

The half-asleep start up wi' fear,
An' think they hear it roaran,
When presently it does appear,
'Twas but some neebor snoran
Asleep that day.

(The Holy Fair)

huge outdoor celebrations of communion then common in the west of Scotland.

Burns had begun under the pressure of adolescent love as a writer of love songs; under the influence of fits of profound melancholy he had later written (in standard English) gloomy religious, moralizing and sometimes melodramatic verses; excited by the religious controversies that went on around him and by what he considered the persecution by the orthodox of his friend Gavin Hamilton, he had then embarked on religious satire; and at this time he was also writing in a form that Scottish poetry had, during the previous seventy-five years, made peculiarly its own – the verse letter, in which, with marvellous skill, he combined formality of stanza and informality of tone, personal feeling and general observation, and an air of impromptu composition with a finely articulated structure.

First Commonplace Book

Between April 1783 and October 1785 Burns kept a Commonplace Book in which he entered poems as well as observations about life and literature. It opens with the unpretentious little song to Nelly Kirkpatrick, followed by a 'Criticism on the foregoing Song'. In March 1784 he copied in some gloomy melodramatic lines entitled *A penitential thought, in the hour of Remorse*, which he later noted were 'intended for a tragedy'. In the same month he noted that he often 'coveted the acquaintance' of people stigmatized as blackguards and prodigals, for he had found among them 'in not a few instances, some of the noblest Virtues, Magnanimity, Generosity, disinterested friendship and even modesty, in the highest perfection'. In April he talked of his melancholy and of the sad pleasure he took in the season of winter, and copied in a song of winter melancholy to be sung to the tune of

34

'McPherson's Farewell'. Then suddenly, after this gloomy and pious poem and in the same month, we get a swinging, rollicking song in the folk tradition, described apologetically as 'a wild Rhapsody, miserably defficient in Versification, but as the sentiments are the genuine feelings of my heart, for that reason I have a particular pleasure in conning it over'. It opens:

> *My father was a farmer upon the Carrick border O*
> *And carefully he bred me, in decency and order O. . . .*

The next entry is a song, *My Nannie, O*, prefaced by some rather pretentious observations about the importance of 'distinguishing foppery & conceit, from real passion & nature'. In August we get *Green grow the rashes, O* and more pretentious reflections on 'the grand end of human life'. Melancholy religious musings, songs (one of them bawdy) and the ballad *John Barleycorn* takes us up to June 1785, when we find *The Death and Dying Words of Poor Mailie*, a mock testament of a dying pet ewe in the old Scottish tradition of animal poetry. Then two splendid verse letters to John Lapraik, an elderly rustic bard, followed by his version of a traditional theme, *Man was Made to Mourn*. The last entry, in October 1785, showed that he had his eye on posterity:

'If ever any young man, on the vestibule of the world, chance to throw his eye over these pages, let him pay a warm attention to the following observations; as I assure him they are the fruit of a poor devil's dear bought Experience. . . .'

Cowgate, Mauchline, where the Armour family lived.

35

Burns and Jean Armour   After recommending 'a regular warm intercourse with the Deity', the manuscript stops abruptly. By now Burns's poetic output was far too great to be accommodated in occasional entries in a Commonplace Book. And he had other things on his mind. He was deeply involved with Jean Armour, the pretty and vivacious daughter of a master mason of Mauchline. Jean became pregnant early in 1786 (she bore twins in September) and Burns was prepared for marriage. In Scots law, consummation followed by declaration of intention to marry constituted legal marriage, and Burns gave Jean a paper which almost certainly was a valid marriage contract. But the Armours were horrified to find their daughter pregnant, and by an impoverished young farmer who enjoyed a reputation for rebelliousness and even blasphemy. Mr Armour compelled his daughter to give up the paper and he had the Ayr lawyer, Robert Aiken, cut out the names of the two parties from the document – an act which made no legal difference to the situation at all, since marriage by declaration was sufficient, but which may have appeased James Armour's rage. But Burns was hurt and indignant at Jean's yielding up the paper, and took it as renunciation of him on her part. And he was deeply indignant that the Armours would rather see their daughter bear an illegitimate child than have her married to him. Further, what he called 'the holy beagles' were after him. However, yielding to what he called 'the rules of the Church' and doing public penance

Presbyterian Penance. 'I have already appeared publicly in Church. . . . Jean and her friends insisted much that she should stand along with me in the kirk, but the minister would not allow it.' (Burns to David Brice, 17 July 1786)

Letter to John Richmond, 9 July 1786, in which Burns refers to his public penance and also to his forthcoming book of poems.

for fornication would get him a certificate as a bachelor, and in his present mood this is what he wanted. Both Robert and Jean appeared three times in church to receive public reproof for the sin of fornication ('I am so far indulged as to appear in my own seat', wrote Robert to a friend), and after their third appearance, on 6 August, Robert was a free man.

But he was a far from happy man. Throughout the crisis with Jean and her parents he had been prey to violently alternating moods. He sought comfort in the arms of Mary Campbell (the 'Highland Mary' of Burns legend), about whom we know very little, and she too may have borne Burns a child; she certainly died, perhaps in childbirth, in October 1786, and in later years he felt terrible pangs of guilt about her. But he could not forget Jean. In June he wrote to a friend:

'I have tryed to forget her: I have run into all kinds of dissipation and riot, Mason-meetings, drinking matches, and other mischief, to drive her out of my head, but all is in vain: and now for a grand cure: the Ship is on her way home that is to take me out to Jamaica; and then, farewell dear old Scotland, and farewell, dear ungrateful Jean, for never, never will I see you more!'

He was in deep trouble. James Armour was trying to enforce payment from Burns for the upkeep of Jean's unborn child, and he feared imprisonment if he could not pay. His friends John Richmond (whom he first met when Richmond was a clerk

37

in Gavin Hamilton's office and who was now a solicitor's clerk in Edinburgh) and James Smith (a Mauchline draper), with whom he had formed 'a happy triumvirate in village revelry' that took pleasure in giving scandal to the orthodox, were now the recipients of desperate letters. To Richmond he wrote on 30 July:

'Would you believe it? Armour has got a warrant to throw me in jail till I find security for an enormous sum. – This they keep an entire secret, but I got it by a channel they little dream of; I am wandering from one friend's house to another, and like a true son of the Gospel "have nowhere to lay my head". – I know you will pour an execration on her head, but spare the poor, ill-advised girl for my sake; tho', may all the Furies that rend the injured, enraged Lover's bosom, await the old harridan, her Mother, untill her latest hour! . . .'

To Smith he wrote about the same time: 'Against two things however, I am fix'd as Fate: staying at home, and owning her [Jean] conjugally. – The first, by Heaven I will not do! the last, by Hell I will never do!' But he concluded: 'If you see Jean tell her, I will meet her, So help me Heaven in my hour of need!' He tried to put his property out of the reach of James Armour by legally assigning his share in the Mossgiel farm to Gilbert for the support of his daughter by Bessie Paton. He talked determinedly of emigration to Jamaica, writing melodramatically to Richmond: 'You and I will never meet in Britain more. – I have orders within three weeks at farthest to repair aboard the Nancy, Cap^n Smith, from Clyde to Jamaica, and to call at Antigua.' It is difficult to know how serious Burns was about emigration. He talked almost hysterically about emigrating but kept postponing his passage. The *Nancy* sailed without him, and so did the *Bell*, on which he next booked passage. In October he wrote to Robert Aiken that he was considering trying to get a job in the Excise service. He added:

'There are many things plead strongly against it; the uncertainty of getting soon

Advertisement for the sailing of the *Nancy*.

For SAVANNAH-LA-MAR, JAMAICA,
To call at ANTIGUA,

THE Brigantine NANCY, ANDREW SMITH, Master, will be at Greenock ready to take in goods, 25th instant, and will be clear to sail by 10th August. For freight or passage, apply to James Brown, insurance-broker, Glasgow, or to the Master at Greenock.
Glasgow, 12th July, 1786.

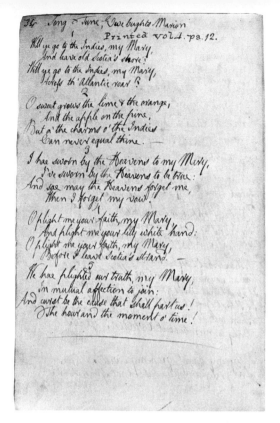

Will ye go to the Indies, my Mary.
Song written for Mary Campbell
when Burns was contemplating
emigration to the West Indies.

into business; the consequences of my follies which may perhaps make it impractic-
able for me to stay at home; and besides I have for some time been pining under
secret wretchedness, from causes which you pretty well know – the pang of disappointment, the sting of pride, with some wandering stabs of remorse, which never
fail to settle on my vitals like vultures, when attention is not called away by the
calls of society, or the vagaries of the Muse. Even in the hour of social mirth,
my gaiety is the madness of the intoxicated criminal under the hands of the
executioner. . . .'

Were these stabs of remorse the result of Mary Campbell's death in bearing a still-
born child of his? The language certainly suggests deep feelings of guilt. We can
only guess. But at any rate his simultaneous emotional involvement with two
women, his ambivalent feelings about Jean, James Armour's threatening attitude,
and his own manic-depressive temperament, were causing him trouble enough.

Something else, however, was also happening. In the deed of assignment in
favour of Elizabeth Paton, written on 30 July with the preamble 'whereas I intend
to leave Scotland and go abroad', he also assigned to her the copyright of his
'Poems presently in the Press'. In early April he had concluded arrangements with
the Kilmarnock printer John Wilson for bringing out a volume of 'Scotch Poems'.

The Kilmarnock volume

39

In his letter to Dr Moore he wrote: 'Before leaving my native country for ever, I resolved to publish my Poems. – I weighed my productions as impartially as in my power; I thought they had merit; and 'twas a delicious idea that I would be called a clever fellow, even though it should never reach my ears a poor Negro-driver, or perhaps a victim to that inhospitable clime gone to the world of Spirits.' But it seems clear that he had arranged for the publication of his poems before he had formed any serious intention of emigrating – if indeed the intention was ever serious. The latter half of 1785 and the early months of 1786 were a period of brilliant and prolific output, and Burns thought well of his own productions. 'I can truly say that pauvre Inconnu as I then was, I had pretty nearly as high an idea of myself and my works as I have at this moment', he wrote in August 1787, some time after his triumphant visit to Edinburgh.

Whatever the immediate spur that led him to publication, the volume duly appeared on 31 July 1786. The title-page read: *Poems, Chiefly in the Scottish Dialect, by Robert Burns*. This is the famous Kilmarnock edition, now one of the most valuable books in the world. Its publication radically changed Burns's life, for its success was immediate and overwhelming. The Reverend George Lawrie, minister in the nearby parish of Loudon, sent a copy to Edinburgh, where it was acclaimed by the *literati*, that group of enlightened men of letters who were making Edinburgh an internationally known intellectual centre. The influential blind poet and critic Dr Thomas Blacklock and the famous philosopher Professor Dugald Stewart were both impressed, and Blacklock wrote to Lawrie on 4 September to say so. Lawrie gave the letter to Gavin Hamilton, who showed it to Burns, who was of course proud and delighted. The local rebel who recited his satirical poems to his country friends had suddenly become a Scottish national poet. And it was not only the *literati* who enjoyed the poems: the book found equal favour in all ranks of society; it was snapped up in farmhouses and cottages as well as in country houses and Edinburgh salons. The Edinburgh salons beckoned him, and on 27 November 1786 Burns set out for the capital to follow up his literary success with a personal appearance.

What sort of poems were in the Kilmarnock volume, and how did Burns come to write them? With what literary tradition was he working and where did he acquire the appropriate skills? To answer these questions, which are crucial for an understanding of Burns's achievement, we must understand something of the Scottish literary tradition as Burns encountered it and of its relation to the English literary tradition of which alone his formal education had taken cognizance.

Burns and the Scottish Literary tradition

As Scottish nationality developed in the early Middle Ages, the languages of Scotland settled down into two: Scots, originally identical with the Anglian speech of northern England, and the Celtic language we now know as Scottish Gaelic. By the fifteenth century, when the stage of Scots we call Middle Scots

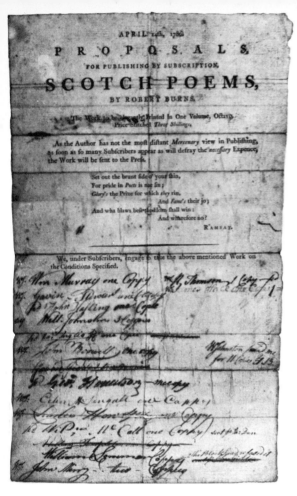

Proposals, for publishing by
subscription, *Scotch Poems* by Robert
Burns. Printed advertisement with the
signatures of the subscribers, 14 April
1786.

View of Kilmarnock.

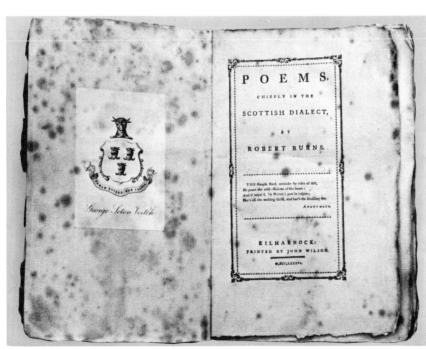

Title-page of the Kilmarnock edition of
Burns's poems.

41

had developed, Scotland was an independent kingdom with a vigorous Middle Scots literature. That literature was naturally influenced by the neighbouring literature of England, especially of Chaucer, but at the same time it had its own national characteristics and its own strong ties with continental European, especially French, literature, France being the traditional ally of Scotland against the common enemy, England. But the Reformation turned Scotland, or at least non-Gaelic-speaking Scotland, more and more towards England; with both England and Scotland officially Protestant and France remaining Catholic this re-alignment became inevitable. John Knox's *History of the Reformation in Scotland*, written in the 1560s, uses a deliberately Anglicized Scots. The translation of the Bible into English made by English Protestant exiles in Geneva in 1560 (when officially England had temporarily reverted to Catholicism under Mary), known as the Geneva Bible, was popular in Scotland and helped to condition Scotsmen to regard English rather than Scots as their literary language. When Queen Elizabeth died in 1603 she was succeeded on the English throne by James VI of Scotland, who now also became James I of England, and on moving to England to take up his new and more powerful position he took with him most of the Court poets and musicians of Scotland. Scotland was too poor a country to afford rich 'Great House' patronage of the arts, as was found in England, and was largely dependent on the Court for artistic patronage. With the disappearance of the Scottish Court, that patronage also disappeared, and Scottish writers were encouraged to write in English for an English audience. Bit by bit the rich language of such great Middle Scots poets as Robert Henryson and William Dunbar broke down into a series of regional dialects, with writers turning more and more to English as their medium. The Union of Parliaments in 1707, which united England and Scotland in an 'incorporating union' and did away with the independent Scottish Parliament, hastened this development. Scots, once a literary language of high potential, became a vernacular, with no literary standard; more and more it came to be used in comic poetry, in condescending jocular imitations of popular verse or serious imitators of ballads, or in antiquarian reconstructions and exercises.

The Union of 1707, removing at a stroke the political independence of the Scottish nation, prompted a nationalist literary reaction that took two forms. The first was nostalgic and in some degree antiquarian. Scotsmen looked back to that phase of their history when their country was free and independent and they had a great literature in their own Scots language. This movement began with James Watson, who between 1706 and 1711 produced his *Choice Collection of Comic and Serious Scots Poems both Ancient and Modern*, a very miscellaneous anthology which represented with some accuracy the different kinds of material available for the development or reconstruction of the Scottish poetic tradition in the eighteenth century. Between 1724 and 1737 Allan Ramsay published his four-

The Gaberlunzie Man, or James V in disguise. The 'Gaberlunzie Man' (a wandering beggar) is a familiar figure in Scottish folklore. There is a tradition that James V (1513–42) liked to wander among his subjects disguised as a beggar.

volume *Tea-Table Miscellany*, a mixed collection of old and new Scottish songs and ballads by authors living and dead, known and unknown. His anthology *The Evergreen* (1724) contained older Scottish poetry, including poems by Henryson and Dunbar. Ramsay's original poetry was often facile and vulgar, but in occasional lyrics, in vigorous poems of Edinburgh low life, and in his dramatic pastoral *The Gentle Shepherd* he showed that he could use Scots with conviction. By now, too, interest in Scottish popular song, a widespread musical form which had replaced the now lost Scottish Court music and which survived, in however attenuated and mutilated a form, the disapproval of Calvinists, was growing among both gentle and simple, and there were many collections of such songs, often with the music, from the *Orpheus Caledonius* of 1726 (published in London) to James Johnson's *Scots Musical Museum* to which, as we shall see, Burns made the major contribution. Of collections of Scots songs without the music, the most important was David Herd's *Ancient and Modern Scots Songs* (second enlarged edition, 1776), which preserved, with a faithfulness to the original texts (even when existing only in fragments) of which Ramsay had been innocent, a large number of what survived of the Scottish folk tradition. Throughout the century ladies and gentlemen amused themselves and their friends by producing imitations of old Scots songs and ballads, sometimes producing intolerably genteel versions

Entry of Prince Charles and the Highlanders into Edinburgh after the Battle of Prestonpans, 1745. ▶

POEMS

By

ROBERT FERGUSSON

EDINBURGH.
Printed by Walter & Thomas Ruddiman.
MDCCLXXIII.

Poems by Robert Fergusson. Title-page of 1773 edition, the only volume of Fergusson's work published in his short lifetime.

of lively older works, but sometimes catching the spirit of the original very effectively. The failure of the Jacobite Rebellion of 1745 gave a new impetus to Scottish folk song by providing a new folk theme, the fate of Bonnie Prince Charlie, the loyalty of his followers and their sorrows in defeat. Another strand in vernacular Scots literature derived from a poem entitled *The Life and Death of the Piper of Kilbarchan, or the Epitaph of Habbie Simson*, a half-comic epitaph and celebration of popular revelry written in Scots by Robert Sempill of Beltrees in the middle of the seventeenth century. This used the stanza now known as the 'Burns stanza' (six lines, with the fourth and sixth lines rhyming and shorter than the other four, which also rhyme). Printed in Watson's collection, the poem was much imitated in the eighteenth century.

This movement, partly popular and partly antiquarian, could not re-create a full-blooded Scots literary language. The Scots poems it produced were self-consciously vernacular poems, written deliberately in the language of the man in the street or on the farm. But Robert Fergusson, an Edinburgh poet of Aberdeenshire parents educated in Dundee and St Andrews, was able to combine the spoken Scots of Edinburgh and of the north-east with more literary elements and fuse them in the light of his own educated sensibility. His Scots poems, contributed

46

to *Ruddiman's Weekly Magazine* in 1772 and 1773, rendered the life of Edinburgh with remarkable warmth and colour and almost succeeded in giving to the Scots vernacular the status of a full literary language. Fergusson died young in 1774; if he had lived he might well have been twinned with Burns, or perhaps even exceeded him, as a Scottish national poet. It was Burns's discovery of Fergusson's poems that stirred him to enthusiasm about the possibilities of Scots poetry and excited him to emulation.

The second kind of nationalist literary reaction that followed on the Union of 1707 went in a quite different direction. Instead of trying to recover and revive the forms and the language of older Scottish literature, the writers in this group strove to write in pure standard English and to prove to England and to Europe that the inhabitants of Scotland could represent Britain in the world of the arts and sciences at least as well as the English. Though patriotic in their own way, they despised their own vernacular Scottish speech and tried to make their writing uncontaminated by what one of them called 'Scotticisms'. These were the *literati* of the Scottish Enlightenment: historians, philosophers, scientists, architects, whose greatest representative is probably the philosopher David Hume. They were very Scottish (Hume was intensely so), yet where the written language was concerned they deliberately chose standard English, regarding their native tongue as a corrupt form of English. They were successful in many fields, but not in poetry, since poetry demands that the whole man speak and therefore requires a language which, however different from the spoken vernacular, is not deliberately cut off from it.

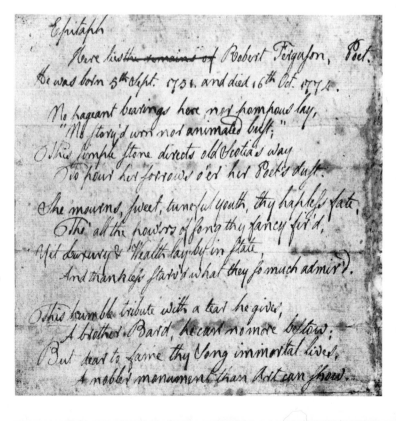

Epitaph for Fergusson by Burns. In 1787 Burns, at his own expense, erected a stone on Fergusson's grave in Canongate parish cemetery. He wrote as an inscription the first four lines of the poem shown here.

In writing of the parish of Mauchline in Volume II of the *Statistical Account of Scotland* (1792), the parish minister, the Reverend William Auld (that same 'Daddy' Auld whom Burns ran afoul of), remarked that 'the Scots dialect is the language spoken, but is gradually improving, and approaching nearer to the English'. In 1787 – the very year when Burns was in Edinburgh – the minor Scottish poet and philosopher James Beattie published his *Scotticisms, Arranged in Alphabetical Order, Designed to Correct Improprieties of Speech and Writing*, thus attesting to the desire of the Scottish *literati* to rid themselves of their Scottish language. We have seen that all of Burns's formal education in literature was entirely and exclusively English. The Scottish part of his literary education he acquired either from the folk tradition, orally, or from the collections of Ramsay and Herd and, most of all, from the example of Fergusson. There were also the chapbooks, sold by itinerant pedlars, which preserved in texts of varying degrees of corruption and modernization a remarkably miscellaneous collection of poetry, tracts, sermons, histories, and other literary and sub-literary forms.

Burns could have accepted the canons of the *literati* and made his bow as a poet in neo-classic English. He had already written several poems in this idiom, and indeed he included some in the Kilmarnock volume – *Despondency, An Ode*, for example, or *The Lament Occasioned by the Unfortunate Issue of A Friend's Amour*. These are full of

Page from James Beattie: *Scotticisms*, 1787.

Letter to William Nicol, 1 June 1787. This is the only extant example of a letter by Burns written throughout in colloquial Ayrshire Scots, and gives a vivid impression of the language he used in talking with his close friends in Ayrshire.

If I fall into the river *I will* be drowned.—I ſhall be drowned. The Scotch phraſe implies, I am *reſolved* or *willing* to be drowned. "If you fall into the water you will be drowned," is right.—*I'll not want*, (Scotch 23d Pſalm),—I ſhall not want. *I'll* is an abreviation of *I will*; and therefore *I'll not want* means, in the Eng. idiom, I am reſolved or determined not to want.—It is not eaſy to give *rules* for the right uſe of *ſhall* and *will*. The following remarks may deſerve a Scotchman's notice.

1. *I will*, and *thou wilt*, ſometimes denote *ſimple volition*, without reference to futurity. If *thou wilt* (art willing), thou canſt make me clean. *I will*; be thou clean.

the poetic clichés of the period, and if Burns had written consistently in this style he would have been remembered, if at all, as a very minor eighteenth-century English versifier. On the other hand, Burns's knowledge of English poetry, especially of eighteenth-century English poetry, served him in good stead. He learned much from Pope's wit and polish and (not always so happily) from Gray's meditative plangency. From the beginning he was a poetic craftsman, not simply a sensitive peasant who burst into verse spontaneously when the spirit moved him. His letters reveal the most precise concern with the wording and the rhythms of his songs, and it is clear that his satiric, epistolary and narrative poetry must have been produced equally conscientiously.

If Burns in the Kilmarnock volume rejected, for the most part, the canons of the *literati*, this does not mean that he rushed headlong to the other extreme to produce a vernacular poetry based entirely on the spoken Scots of the Ayrshire countryside. He learned from Fergusson to produce his own combination of Scots and English, of the colloquial and the literary. Sometimes he uses an English just tipped with Scots, sometimes the Scots element is more pronounced, sometimes it is overwhelming. His idiom is flexible, adaptable to different subjects and different moods. But in general he presents himself as a Scottish poet and the poems as 'Scotch Poems'. In his printed proposals for publishing his poems he quotes a belligerent verse by Allan Ramsay, written in ripe Scots, announcing the right of poets to be proud.

He chose the poems for the Kilmarnock volume with care. He did not wish to *Début as poet* give offence to the *literati*, even though he did not adopt their attitude to language. He omitted the *Twa Herds*, that rollicking ecclesiastical satire, as well as *The Ordination*, another anti-clerical poem of more purely local interest. He omitted a lively satire on the Tarbolton schoolmaster, *Death and Doctor Hornbook*. More surprisingly, he omitted the *Address to the Unco Guid*, a warning against complacency and censoriousness which could hardly have given offence. And he omitted one of his greatest poems, the magnificent satire on Calvinism, *Holy Willie's Prayer*. Finally, he omitted *The Jolly Beggars*, that extraordinary anarchistic 'cantata', said to be based on his observation of carousing beggars at Poosie Nansie's, the Mauchline pub he frequented.

But what he included was remarkable enough. The volume opens with *The Twa Dogs*, a poem in the old Scottish animal tradition in which the dialogue between a rich man's and a poor man's dog in lively octosyllabic couplets produces social satire that is both comic and biting. He follows it with a poem in praise of whisky, *Scotch Drink*, written in the 'Burns stanza': here he deftly combines bacchanalian celebration and pungent social comment, without at any point doing violence to the general mood of conviviality. Another poem on whisky follows, and then comes the magnificent *Holy Fair*, in which he uses an old Scots stanza with remarkable skill. Next comes the *Address to the Deil*, in which he handles that formidable character

49

Poor Mailie. Woodcut by Thomas Bewick from the 1814 edition of Burns's poems.

with an almost affectionate familiarity which has its own kind of irony. *The Death and Dying Words of Poor Mailie* and *Poor Mailie's Elegy*, which follow, are splendid examples of Burns's handling of the seventeenth-century Scottish poetic tradition of the mock testament and the mock elegy on an animal (Mailie was a pet ewe). Then we have the verse letter to James Smith, the first of seven verse letters in the volume which show Burns's remarkable skill in this difficult form. He begins by setting the scene as he sits and writes – the place, the season of the year indicated with precise agricultural references – then he moves out from his own position to generalizations about life which are, however, never vapid or sententious but always directly linked to the personal situation he has been describing; then the poet links his correspondent's situation with his own, and after any of a variety of developments returns to himself writing and signs off with grace and adroitness. Burns's verse letters are among the very finest of his poems.

There follows *A Dream*, a birthday address to the King in mingled tones of respect, avuncular advice and reproof which does not quite come off (it gave some offence to Burns's genteel friends). *The Vision* follows: it begins splendidly in a rich Scots, but when it moves into a rather pretentious neo-classic English it becomes stilted and less convincing. *Hallowe'en* is a description of country Hallowe'en customs with an almost antiquarian or anthropological insistence on detail and a heavy use of rustic Scots. Another animal poem is *The Auld Farmer's New-Year-Morning Salutation to his Auld Mare, Maggie*, in which the mare is treated as a fellow worker with an effective combination of humour and sentiment. Then comes what the Edinburgh *literati* regarded as the prize of the volume, *The Cotter's Saturday Night*, which shows the influence of Gray's *Elegy* as well as of its model, Fergusson's fine poem *The Farmer's Ingle* [fireside]. Its opening dedicatory stanza (addressed to the Ayr lawyer Robert Aiken, the same man who cut out the names from Jean Armour's marriage document) is stilted and pretentious; its second stanza is magnificent, and shows an interesting combination of English and Scottish influences; the rest of the poem alternates a beautifully etched Dutch interior with moral generalizations enunciated in a high rhetorical manner which sometimes ring very hollow indeed. Then comes the most popular of all Burns's animal poems, *To a Mouse*, where he avoids sentimentality by his faithfulness to the agricultural facts, his unaffected fellow-feeling for the mouse, and his ability to link skilfully and without moral gesturing the fates 'of mice and men'.

Of the other poems in the Kilmarnock volume, some, like *To Ruin*, are rhetorical and sentimental and in standard English; one, *To a Louse, on Seeing one on a Lady's Bonnet at Church*, is an outstanding example of Burns's ability to treat a trivial subject humorously yet in such a way as to set going impressive moral reverberations; four are songs, of which only the first, *It was upon a Lammas night*, shows anything of Burns's true genius in this form; and the rest include a *Dedication* to Gavin Hamilton (interestingly enough, not put first), some indifferent *Epitaphs and Epigrams*, and a sententious (and purely English) *Bard's Epitaph*. There is also *To a Mountain-Daisy*, where he attempts to repeat the success of *To a Mouse*, but unsuccessfully, for self-conscious sensibility takes over and ousts that special sense of reality which provides the groundwork of all Burns's best poems. It is written mostly in standard neoclassic English, and was much admired by the *literati*.

If we take together the best poems in the Kilmarnock volume and the poems he had already written but which he omitted from the volume, we see at once that by 1786 Burns had, without ever leaving his native Ayrshire or giving up his arduous life as a working farmer, developed into a remarkable poet. Indeed, except for the songs, to which he devoted the last years of his life, and his one narrative poem, the

Manuscript of *The Cotter's Saturday Night*, showing the quotation from Gray's *Elegy*, used as an epigraph. (Right) A page from William Burnes's Bible which is referred to in the poem.

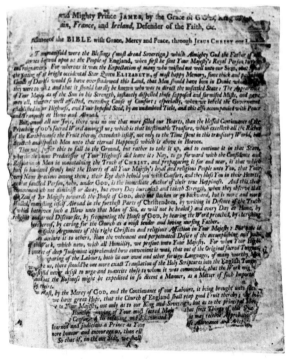

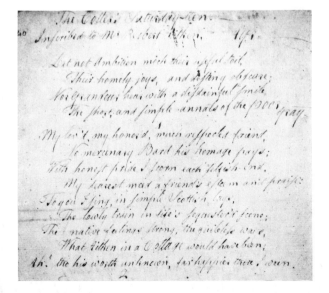

Tam o' Shanter at Alloway Kirk. Wash drawing by Alexander Carse.

splendid *Tam o' Shanter*, nothing that he was to write later really enhances his reputation. He was already a skilled and mature poet, deftly combining Scottish and
English elements to produce a poetry which at its best and most characteristic is
solidly grounded in experience yet is not merely descriptive or merely autobiographical; it is a poetry wrung from life yet – even in its most bitterly satiric moments –
celebratory of life, often a poetry in which the irony, as in *The Holy Fair*, is not only
consistent with but actually arises from his acceptance of the incorrigible absurdities
of the human condition.

In his Preface to the Kilmarnock volume Burns deliberately exaggerated his lack
of education and played up to the sentimental notion of the 'natural man', the
primitive poet of Nature, that certain members of the *literati* had discussed in their
writings. For there is a paradox in the fact that while the *literati* held to standards of
neo-classic elegance in their practical criticism, they at the same time professed a
belief in natural genius. In their literary criticism they traced the origin of poetry to
spontaneous emotional speech. Indeed, the concern with primitive poetry shown

by the Edinburgh *literati* is one of their most interesting features, and has links with later developments in the Romantic movement. But Burns was not a primitive poet, for all his protestations; he was sophisticated and skilled, and he knew what he was doing. He also knew just what he was doing when he wrote in his Preface:

'The following trifles are not the production of the Poet, who with all the advantages of learned art, and perhaps amid the elegancies and idlenesses of upper life, looks down for a rural theme, with an eye to Theocrites (*sic*) or Virgil. To the Author of this, these and other celebrated names their countrymen are, in their original languages, "A fountain shut up, and a book sealed". Unacquainted with the necessary requisites for commencing Poet by rule, he sings the sentiments and manners, he felt and saw in himself and his rustic compeers around him, in his and their native language.'

But though he presents himself as an unlettered rustic, he also shows his pride:
'To his Subscribers, the Author returns his most sincere thanks. Not the mercenary bow over a counter, but the heart-throbbing gratitude of the Bard, conscious how much he is indebted to Benevolence and Friendship, for gratifying him, if he deserves it, in that dearest wish of every poetic bosom – to be distinguished. . . .'

Part of the Preface to the Edinburgh edition of the poems, 1787.

(vi)

their Ancestors?—The Poetic Genius of my Country found me as the prophetic bard Eli-jah did Elisha—at the plough; and threw her inspiring mantle over me. She bade me sing the loves, the joys, the rural scenes and rural pleasures of my natal Soil, in my native tongue: I tuned my wild, artless notes, as she inspired.—She whispered me to come to this ancient metropolis of Cale-donia, and lay my Songs under your honour-ed protection: I now obey her dictates.

Though much indebted to your goodness, I do not approach you, my Lords and Gentle-men, in the usual stile of dedication, to thank you for past favours; that path is so hack-neyed by prostituted Learning, that honest Rusticity is ashamed of it.—Nor do I pre-sent this Address with the venal soul of a servile Author, looking for a continuation of those favours: I was bred to the Plough, and am independent. I come to claim the common Scottish name with you, my illustri-ous

(vii)

...us Countrymen; and to tell the world that I glory in the title.—I come to congratulate my Country, that the blood of her ancient heroes still runs uncontaminated; and that from your courage, knowledge, and public spirit, she may expect protection, wealth, and liberty.—In the last place, I come to proffer my warmest wishes to the Great Fountain of Honour, the Monarch of the Universe, for your welfare and happiness.

When you go forth to waken the Echoes, in the ancient and favourite amusement of your Forefathers, may Pleasure ever be of your party; and may Social-joy await your re-turn! When harassed in courts or camps with the justlings of bad men and bad mea-sures, may the honest consciousness of injured Worth attend your return to your native Seats; and may Domestic Happiness, with a smiling welcome, meet you at your gates! May Corruption shrink at your kindling in-dignant glance; and may tyranny in the Ruler

The literary men of Edinburgh took Burns's primitivist claims literally. The Reviewer in *The Edinburgh Magazine* of October 1786 referred to him as 'a striking example of native genius bursting through the obscurity of poverty and the obstructions of laborious life' and admired 'the exertions of untutored fancy' in the poems. *The Monthly Review* of December talked of 'the humble bard' with 'his simple strains, artless and unadorned' [which] 'seem to flow without effort from the native feelings of the heart'. And the respected and influential Henry Mackenzie, writing in the December issue of his periodical *The Lounger*, hailed Burns as a 'Heaven-taught ploughman' and noted the 'uncommon penetration and sagacity' with which he had observed men and manners 'from his humble and unlettered station'. Mackenzie admired *To a Mountain-Daisy*, which he quoted in full, and he praised the 'solemn and sublime' poems of 'rapt and sublime melancholy' (such as *Despondency* and *Winter, A Dirge*) which seem to us to be unimpressive rhetorical exercises in a tradition with which the poet was not inward. He also singled out *The Cotter's Saturday Night* and *To a Mouse*, and he defended Burns against the objection that some of his poems breathed 'a spirit of libertinism and irreligion' by arguing that the poet was understandably against the pernicious narrowness bred by 'the ignorance and fanaticism of the lower class of people' without being an 'enemy of religion', though he thought that his Muse had 'sometimes been a little unguarded in her ridicule of hypocrisy'. He conceded that Burns sometimes offended against delicacy, but added: 'When we reflect on his rank in life, the habits to which he must have been subject, and the society in which he must have mixed, we regret perhaps more than wonder, that delicacy should be so often offended in perusing a volume in which there is so much to interest and to please us.' But most important of all, he described Burns unequivocally as 'a genius of no ordinary rank' and ended with a plea to the wealthy and influential 'to repair the wrongs of suffering or neglected merit; to call forth genius from the obscurity in which it had pined indignant, and place it where it may profit or delight the world'.

Opening paragraph from the review of the poems, in the *Monthly Review*, December 1786.

ART. V. *Poems, chiefly in the Scottish Dialect.* By Robert Burns. 8vo. Kilmarnock printed. No Bookseller's Name, nor Price. 1786.

POETA nascitur, non fit, is an old maxim, the truth of which has been generally admitted; and although it be certain that in modern times many verses are manufactured from the brain of their authors with as much labour as the iron is drawn into form under the hammer of the smith, and require to be afterwards smoothed by the file with as much care as the burnishers

Ff 4   of

Henry Mackenzie (1745–1831). This portrait, by Colvin Smith, shows Mackenzie in old age, when he had long been a dominating figure in Edinburgh literary life.

Mackenzie's plea for influential patronage for Burns went unanswered, for all the adulation with which Burns was showered in Edinburgh, and it was probably as well, for the well-meaning advice that the influential critics gave to Burns ran quite counter to the set of his genius. They would have had him write elegantly senti-mental poems in a neo-classic English which he could handle effectively in poetry only when leavened with Scots or when put at the service of an attitude of mind that would have much disturbed the *literati*. They advised him to handle themes from classical mythology and expected him to learn to follow the approved poetic fashions of the time with docility and gratitude for advice. At the same time, however, most of them did admire his originality, his unique kind of vitality, and the authenticity of the rustic background out of which his poems sprang. (James Beattie in Aberdeen was one who did not share this admiration. He wrote proudly of his son that 'he was early warned against the use of Scotch words and other similar improprieties; and his dislike to them was such, that he soon learned to avoid them; and, after he grew up, could never endure to read what was written in any of the vulgar dialects of Scotland'.)

Burns's immediate intention in setting out for Edinburgh on 27 November 1786 was to arrange for the publication there of a second edition of his poems and to see what the prospects were of a job for him in the Excise, then a common way of pro-viding for deserving characters of small means. And of course he also wanted to

Burns in Edinburgh

Edinburgh from St Anthony's Chapel. This ruined fifteenth-century hermitage and chapel commands a fine view of the city. Shown here are the Old Town on the left and part of the early New Town on the right.

meet the *literati*, whose approval flattered and cheered him but with respect to whom he remained touchily on the defensive. He spent the first night at the farm of Covington Mains, near Biggar, Lanarkshire, as the guest of the farmer, Archibald Prentice, who made 'a most agreeable little party' for him, as Burns wrote to his friend George Reid of Barquharie (from whom he had borrowed a horse for the journey). The next night he also spent at a farmhouse, and the following afternoon he arrived at Edinburgh to lodge in Baxter's Close, Lawnmarket, with his old friend John Richmond who had rented a room there from a Mrs Carfrae.

Baxter's Close was, like all the Edinburgh 'closes', a narrow street flanked by high flats; it was in the heart of the Old Town of Edinburgh, running off the Lawnmarket which is at the western end of the wide thoroughfare that runs along the ridge joining the Castle on the west with Holyrood Palace on the east. The Old

Baxter's Close, Edinburgh.

George Square. Built by James Brown in 1766, it shows a movement to develop Edinburgh to the south. The city magistrates disapproved, however, and developed the New Town to the north.

Town was essentially this thoroughfare with its 'closes' and 'wynds' running off at right angles, giving the town the appearance of a herring-bone, but by the time Burns arrived considerable progress had been made in extending the city, first to the south, but more significantly to the north across the valley of the North Loch which was drained between 1759 and 1763 and bridged at its eastern end by 1772. Brown Square and George Square had been built to the south in the 1760s and immediately became fashionable. In the next decade the carefully planned developments to the north of the valley began the creation of the New Town, which was rising rapidly when Burns arrived in the city. The ordered elegance of the streets and squares of the New Town reflected the ideals of the Scottish Enlightenment and the aesthetically tidy minds of the Edinburgh *literati*. But Burns lodged in the Old Town, sharing a bed with his friend Richmond for a rent of eighteenpence a week. It was a crowded and dirty but very romantic part of Edinburgh, with the Castle immediately to the west and Parliament Square and the church of St Giles almost opposite.

Burns had been a Freemason since June 1781, when he was 'entered an appren-tice', in the St David Masonic Lodge of Tarbolton. This provided him with one kind of entrée into Edinburgh society, and soon after his arrival he was introduced to the Canongate Kilwinning Lodge, which numbered some influential persons among its members. He was assumed a member of the lodge the following Febru-ary and, more significantly, at a meeting of the Grand Lodge of Scotland in January he heard the Grand Master give the toast, 'Caledonia, and Caledonia's Bard, Brother Burns'. But his first weeks in Edinburgh were spent meeting all sorts of people and learning how to bear up against every kind of patronizing and con-descending helpfulness. He was also lionized, he was regarded as a phenomenon, people struggled for an opportunity to see and speak with this ploughman genius; it was a testing time for a young man up from the country.

Burns preserved his sense of humour and his sense of proportion. On 7 December he wrote to Gavin Hamilton:

'For my own affairs, I am in a fair way of becoming as eminent as Thomas a Kempis or John Bunyan; and you may expect henceforth to see my birthday inserted among the wonderful events, in the Poor Robin's and Aberdeen Almanacks, along with the black Monday & the battle of Bothwel bridge – My Lord Glencairn & the Dean of Faculty, Mr H. Erskine, have taken me under their wing; and by all probability I shall soon be the tenth Worthy, and the eighth Wise Man, of the world. . . .'

Letter to Gavin Hamilton, 7 December 1786. Written from Edinburgh and showing Burns's characteristic self-mockery about his sensational social success there.

James, Earl of Glencairn. 'The noble Earl of Glencairn, to whom I owe more than to any man of earth, does me the honor of giving me his strictures: his hints, with respect to impropriety or indelicacy, I follow implicitly.' (Burns to Mrs Dunlop, 22 March 1787)

The Earl of Glencairn, who was patron of Kilmarnock parish and whose attention had been drawn to Burns's volume of poems by his factor, Alexander Dalziel, became at once a great admirer of Burns and, as Burns continued in his letter to Gavin Hamilton, it was through Glencairn's influence that 'it is inserted in the records of the Caledonian Hunt, that they universally, one & all, subscribe for the 2d Edition'. On 13 December he wrote to John Ballantine, an Ayr banker who was much interested in Burns's poetic career, that he had been introduced to 'many of the noblesse' and that he numbered the Duchess of Gordon as well as the Earl and Countess of Glencairn among his 'avowed Patrons & Patronesses'. He continued: 'I have likewise warm friends among the Literati, Professors Stewart, Blair [Hugh Blair, Professor of Rhetoric at Edinburgh University and distinguished literary critic], Greenfield [the Reverend William Greenfield, a colleague of Blair's] and Mr McKenzie the Man of feeling'. He concludes his letter by confessing: 'now I tremble lest I should be ruined by being dragged to [*sic*] suddenly into the glare of polite & learned observation'.

Professor Dugald Stewart had invited Burns to dine at his country house near Mauchline in October, before Burns went to Edinburgh, and now he saw much more of him. Years later, when Dr James Currie was preparing his pioneer edition and biography of Burns, Stewart wrote to Currie his impressions of the poet in Edinburgh: 'His manners were then, as they continued ever afterwards, simple, manly, and independent; strongly expressive of conscious genius and worth; but without anything that indicated forwardness, arrogance, or vanity. He took his share in the conversation, but not more than belonged to him; and listened with apparent attention and deference, on subjects where his want of education deprived him of the means of information.' He added, significantly: 'If there had been a little more of gentleness and accommodation in his temper, he would, I think, have been still more interesting; but he had been accustomed to give law in the circle of his ordinary acquaintance, and his dread of any thing approaching to meanness or servility, rendered his manner somewhat decided and hard.' Stewart spoke of the 'precision, and originality of his language, when he spoke in company; more particularly as he aimed at purity in his turn of expression, and avoided more successfully than most Scotchmen, the peculiarities of Scottish phraseology'. The poetess and prominent figure of Edinburgh society, Mrs Alison Cockburn, remarked of Burns after he had been in Edinburgh a few weeks: 'The man will be spoiled, if he can spoil, but he keeps his simple manners, and is quite sober.' Dugald Stewart agreed:

'The attentions he received during his stay in town from all ranks and descriptions of persons, were such as would have turned any head but his own. I cannot say that I could perceive any unfavourable effect which they left on his mind. He retained

Professor Dugald Stewart and his family. 'I never spent an afternoon among great folks with half that pleasure as when, in company with you, I had the honor of paying my devoirs to that plain, honest, worthy man, the Professor.' (Burns to Dr Mackenzie, October 1786)

James Burnett, Lord Monboddo, judge and man of letters, was one of the more eccentric of the *literati*.

Elizabeth Burnett, Lord Monboddo's beautiful second daughter, whom Burns much admired. She died in 1790 aged 25.

the same simplicity of manners and appearance which had struck me so forcibly when I first saw him in the country; nor did he seem to feel any additional self-importance from the number and rank of his new acquaintances. His dress was perfectly suited to his station, plain and unpretending, with a sufficient attention to neatness. If I recollect aright, he always wore boots; and, when on more than usual ceremony, buck-skin breeches.'

Those buck-skin breeches were not the habitual dress of an Ayrshire farmer, but the dress, as it were, of an idealized peasant. Burns's dress may have been 'plain and unpretending', but this young man who had once worn the only tied hair in the parish knew exactly what he was doing sartorially. He was also perfectly aware of the risks he was running. In December he wrote to Greenfield:

'Never did Saul's armour sit so heavy on David when going to encounter Goliah, as does the encumbering robe of public notice with which the friendship and patron-age of some "names dear to fame" have invested me. – I do not say this in the ridicul-ous idea of seeming self-abasement, and affected modesty. – I have long studied myself, and I think I know pretty exactly what ground I occupy, both as a Man & a Poet; and however the world, or a friend, may sometimes differ from me in that particular, I stand for it, in silent resolve, with all the tenaciousness of Property. – I am willing to believe that my abilities deserved a better fate than the veriest shades of life; but to be dragged forth, with all my imperfections on my head, to the full glare of learned and polite observation, is what, I am afraid, I shall have bitter reason to repent. –

'I mention this to you, once for all, merely, in the Confessor style, to disburthen my conscience, and that – "When proud fortune's ebbing tide recedes" – you may bear me witness, when my bubble of fame was at the highest, I stood, unintoxicated, with the inebriating cup in my hand, looking forward, with rueful resolve, to the hastening time when the stroke of envious Calumny, with all the eagerness of vengeful triumph, should dash it to the ground. – '

With his busy social life ('No doubt he will be at the Hunters' Ball tomorrow, which has made all women and milliners mad', wrote Mrs Cockburn of him in December) he had little time left for poetry. But he did compose a few pieces. The lively and still popular *Address to a Haggis* appeared in the *Caledonian Mercury* of 19 December and in the *Scots Magazine* for January. Its language is a sprightly Scots, one of the few good poems in that idiom which he wrote at this time. It is in marked contrast to another poem of his, which also appeared in the *Caledonian Mercury*. This was the *Address to Edinburgh*, a duty poem written in gratitude to the Edinburgh *literati* in a style both frigid and pompous. Its opening line, 'Edina! Scotia's darling seat!' is all too revealing. But on the whole Burns resisted the influence of the *literati*.

Party at Lord Monboddo's house. 'His lordship's private life was spent in the enjoyment of domestic felicity and in the practice of all the social virtues. . . . There were few things he so much delighted in as the convivial society of his friends.' (*Kay's Edinburgh Portraits*)

Mrs Dunlop. 'A little, very little while ago, I had scarce a friend but the stubborn pride of my own bosom; now I am distinguished, patronised, befriended by YOU.' (Burns to Mrs Dunlop, 22 March 1787)

'I have the advice of some very judicious friends among the Literati here', he wrote in March 1787 to Mrs Dunlop of Dunlop, a fifty-six-year-old widow who had been redeemed from boredom and depression by reading the Kilmarnock volume and with whom Burns developed a lengthy correspondence, 'but with them I sometimes find it necessary to claim the privilege of thinking for myself'. When in October 1787 Burns visited John Ramsay of Ochtertyre at Harvieston, Clackmannanshire, Ramsay asked Burns 'whether the Literati had mended his poems, by their criticisms'. To which Burns replied: 'Sir, the gentlemen remind me of some spinsters in my country who spin their thread so fine that it is neither fit for weft nor woof.' He added that he had not changed a word except one, to please Dr Blair. (This was probably the change of the line 'Wi' tidings of salvation' to the much more effective 'Wi' tidings o' damnation' in *The Holy Fair*.)

It was unfortunate for Burns that he arrived at Edinburgh in the gap between two periods of Edinburgh's Golden Age, the age of David Hume (who had been dead for ten years) and the age of Scott (who was a youngster of sixteen when he saw Burns at the house of Professor Adam Ferguson). He met no real intellectual challenge. There was no absolutely first-rate mind among the *literati* he met. He himself needed intellectual stimulation as well as a kind of understanding that required more imagination than any of his Edinburgh friends had. For it must be emphasized that Burns was a man of high intellectual gifts. Maria Riddell, the lively and attractive literary lady whom Burns was to know well in the early 1790s, wrote of him after his death that his poetic talents were less than his more general intellectual qualities. 'If others have climbed more successfully the heights of

Parnassus,' she wrote, 'none certainly ever outshone Burns in the charms – the sorcery I would almost call it – of fascinating conversation; the spontaneous eloquence of social argument, or the unstudied poignancy of brilliant repartee. . . . I believe no man was ever gifted with a larger portion of the *vivida vis animi*: the animated expressions of his countenance were almost peculiar to himself. The rapid lightnings of his eye were always the harbingers of some flash of genius, whether they darted the fiery glances of insulted and indignant superiority, or beamed with the impassioned sentiment of fervent and impetuous affections.' Such a man would obviously resent being exhibited like 'the learned pig in the Grassmarket' (as he once contemptuously put it), especially among people of higher social rank to whom he felt himself intellectually superior. In spite or perhaps because of the friends he made among the great and the influential, his pride remained ever on the alert.

It is understandable in the circumstances that he sometimes looked to a less exalted circle for friendship. He made friends with the coarse and irascible but talented and lively William Nicol, who had an unenviable reputation for harshness as a Latin master at the High School of Edinburgh but whom Burns loved for his wit, conviviality and intellectual gaiety. He became a member of the Crochallan

Walter Scott meeting Burns at Sciennes House. Many years later, Scott gave his impression of Burns. 'There was a strong expression of sense and shrewdness in all his lineaments: the eye alone, I think, indicated the poetical character and temperament. It was large, and of a cast which glowed (I say literally *glowed*) when he spoke with feeling or interest.'

Fencibles, the drinking club which met in Anchor Close not far from his lodgings. He was introduced by its founder, the printer William Smellie, and here joined happily in the singing of bawdy songs and the telling of bawdy anecdotes which would have horrified Dr Blacklock and Hugh Blair. This was the Edinburgh that Fergusson had celebrated, not the Edinburgh of the *literati*. Then there was the young Edinburgh law student Robert Ainslie, with whom Burns developed a cheerful intimacy, and Peter Hill, clerk in the office of William Creech the publisher. These too belonged to the lower and gayer Edinburgh world.

The Edinburgh edition

It was the Earl of Glencairn who introduced Burns to Creech, who became Burns's literary agent. A 'Memorandum of Agreement' between Burns and Creech to publish a second edition of the poems was drawn up at Henry Mackenzie's house on 17 April 1787. On Mackenzie's advice, Burns accepted a hundred guineas for the copyright of the poems, but this was in addition to the subscription money. Creech, now owning the copyright, had the right to publish further editions solely

Smellie's printing office. The building survived till 1859.

William Smellie.

Shrewd Willie Smellie to Crochallan came;
The old cock'd hat, the grey surtout, the same;
His bristling beard just rising in its might,
'Twas four long nights and days to shaving night . . .

(Impromptu poem by Burns, 1787)

William Creech. 'I am nearly agreed with Creech to print my book; and, I suppose, I will begin on monday.' (Burns to John Ballantine, 13 December 1786)

for his own benefit. It does not seem to us a very generous arrangement, but Burns was satisfied. It has been calculated that Burns made altogether about £855 from the sale of the subscription copies and the hundred guineas. He had made rather more than fifty pounds from the Kilmarnock volume. This was virtually all he was ever to make from his poetry.

William Smellie was the printer of the new edition, and it was at Smellie's office in Anchor Close that Burns corrected the proofs, sitting on a stool that came to be known as Burns's Stool. The volume – known as the Edinburgh edition – was published on 21 April 1787. It included a dedication 'to the Noblemen and Gentlemen of the Caledonian Hunt' in a high rhetorical style which combined self-assertion, gratitude and Scottish patriotic feeling. '. . . Nor do I present this Address with the venal soul of a servile Author, looking for a continuation of those favours: I was bred to the Plough, and am independant. I come to claim the common Scottish name with you, my illustrious Countrymen; and to tell the world that I glory in the title. – I come to congratulate my Country, that blood of her ancient

Burns's Stool.

67

The 'auld brig', Ayr. It was extensively restored in 1910.

Auld Brig appear'd of ancient Pictish race,
The vera wrinkles Gothic in his face.

(The Brigs of Ayr)

heroes still runs uncontaminated; and that, from your courage, knowledge, and public spirit, she may expect protection, wealth, and liberty.' The new volume also contained a 37-page list of subscribers.

Of the twenty-two poems included in the volume that had not appeared in the Kilmarnock edition, most had been already written before the earlier edition and he included them now because he thought they would please the taste of the Edinburgh gentry and *literati*. Burns included *Death and Doctor Hornbook, The Ordination* and *Address to the Unco Guid*, which he had omitted from the Kilmarnock volume out of caution, though it is difficult to see why they were considered suitable now but not earlier. Five religious poems in somewhat stilted neo-classic English are of little interest. The *Address to Edinburgh* is of course there, as is the *Address to a Haggis*. The most interesting of the added poems is *The Brigs of Ayr*, which had been written in the late summer or early autumn of 1786. This dialogue between the spirits of the old and the new bridges over the Ayr River, written in heroic couplets, combines Scottish and English inspiration. The tradition of a dialogue between inanimate objects Burns got from Fergusson, but the style of parts of the poem owes much to English influences. The opening is in the sententiously reflective style of much mid-eighteenth-century English verse, but when Burns eventually gets the two bridges talking he moves into a racy Scots. The description of the River Ayr in spate, put into the mouth of the auld brig, is a set piece of great virtuosity, comparable to Gavin Douglas's splendid description of winter in the prologue to Book VII of his Middle Scots translation of the *Aeneid*.

The Edinburgh edition also contains five songs, of which one, *Green grow the rashes, O* shows Burns in his best form as a song-writer. He had entered it in his Commonplace Book in August 1784 but had not thought it worth including in the Kilmarnock volume. Songs were not regarded as the highest kind of poetic production by the *literati*, and Burns was chary of including them in his show volumes. But this song shows what Burns could do when following the folk idiom. Like so many of the songs he was later to write, it captures with great precision the passion of the moment, reducing the world to the single experience of sexual love. It is interesting to see how Burns could adapt to the folk idiom a sentiment expressed with neo-classic elegance by Pope. Pope, in the Second Epistle of his *Moral Essays*, had written

> *Heaven, when it strives to polish all it can*
> *Its last best work, but forms a softer Man.*

Burns's song concludes:

> *Auld Nature swears, the lovely Dears*
> *Her noblest work she classes, O:*
> *Her prentice han' she try'd on man,*
> *An' then she made the lasses, O.*

Like all Burns's songs, it is written for a particular air, which it fits perfectly.

It was the Edinburgh edition that established Burns's fame beyond Scotland. It was brought out almost immediately by Cadell and Davis in London; there were pirated editions in Dublin and Belfast; and soon afterwards editions appeared also in Philadelphia and New York. It was by the poems in this volume (that is, those that had appeared in the Kilmarnock edition with the twenty-two additional poems) that Burns was judged in his lifetime.

So Burns achieved one of his aims in coming to Edinburgh: he got a new edition of his poems published there. His other ambition, that of getting a position in the Excise, was not encouraged by his new friends. It was the duty of the Heaven-taught ploughman to stay at the plough. In a sense, Burns was paying the penalty of his own exaggeration of his role as natural genius. A natural genius hardly belonged in the Excise service: he must return to his rustic environment and there warble again his native woodnotes wild. Patrick Miller, an Edinburgh banker who admired Burns's poems, had recently bought Dalswinton estate in the valley of the Nith near Dumfries and offered to lease the poet a farm on it. Burns was not keen. 'Some life-rented, embittering Recollections,' he wrote to John Ballantine, 'whisper me that I will be happier anywhere than in my old neighborhood, but Mr Miller is no Judge of land; and though I dare say he means to favour me, yet he may give me, in his opinion, an advantageous bargain that may ruin me.' Burns's misgivings proved to be only too well founded. In the meantime, he continued his efforts to get an Excise position and postponed a decision on Miller's offer.

Trial of the first steamboat. William Symington's pioneer steamboat was financed by Patrick Miller. It made its first trials on Dalswinton Loch (on Miller's estate) and it is possible that on one occasion Burns was a passenger.

Robert Burns. Miniature
by Alexander Reid,
painted early in 1795.
Burns did not consider it a
good likeness.

As Burns lingered on in Edinburgh he became increasingly aware of the uncertainty of his position. Again and again he mentioned to correspondents that he
was sure that his popularity among the Edinburgh gentry was bound to be temporary. He wrote to Mrs Dunlop in January: '. . . to be dragged forth to the full
glare of learned and polite observation, with all my imperfections of aukward
rusticity and crude unpolished ideas on my head – I assure you, Madam, I do not
dissemble when I tell you I tremble for the consequences. The novelty of a Poet in
my obscure situation, without any of those advantages which are reckoned necessary
for that character, at least at this time of day, has raised a partial tide of public notice
which has borne me to a height, where I am absolutely, feelingly certain my
abilities are inadequate to support me; and too surely do I see that time when the
same tide will leave me, and recede, perhaps, as far below the mark of truth.' He
wrote to the Reverend George Lawrie in February that he knew he owed his
'present eclat' to novelty only, 'but I see the time not distant far when the popular
tide which has borne me to a height of which I am perhaps unworthy shall recede
with silent celerity and leave me a barren waste of sand, to descend at my leisure to
my former station'. Of course he wanted to continue his career as a poet ('The
appellation of, a Scotch Bard, is by far my highest pride; to continue to deserve it is
my most exalted ambition', he wrote to Mrs Dunlop in March), and he wanted to

71

Coldstream Bridge. 'Monday [7 May 1787] – Coldstream – went over to England – Cornhill – glorious river Tweed – clear and majestic – fine bridge.' (Burns's Journal of his Border tour)

travel round Scotland to familiarize himself with Scottish landscape and the land marks of Scottish history. But the economic problem remained. Mrs Dunlop sug gested that he purchase a commission in the army, but this was quite unrealistic advice.

Travels   Burns left Edinburgh on 5 May to travel in the Border country, so rich in historical and literary tradition, before returning to Ayrshire. His friend Bob Ainslie accompanied him much of the way. He crossed briefly into England at Coldstream, then proceeded through the Border towns of Jedburgh, Melrose and Selkirk before turning east and visiting Eyemouth, where the St Abb Masonic Lodge gave him an official welcome. A second crossing into England, this time as far south as New castle, was followed by a westward movement to Carlisle, whence he journeyed back to Scotland, to Dumfries, where he received the freedom of the burgh, and then to look at the farm that Patrick Miller proposed to lease to him. He was back at

Mossgiel on 9 June, a famous poet, but deeply unsettled in mind and quite uncertain about the future.

'I cannot settle to my mind', he wrote to James Smith from Mauchline on 11 June. 'Farming, the only thing of which I know anything, and heaven above knows but little do I understand of that, I cannot, dare not risk on farms as they are. If I do not fix, I will go for Jamaica.' He cannot have been serious about Jamaica. A few days later he met Patrick Miller at Dalswinton and they discussed the farm plan again. They agreed to meet again in August, with nothing yet definitely decided. Meanwhile, he could not return to the Mossgiel routine. He nursed his pride. 'I have bought a pocket Milton,' he wrote to William Nicol on 18 June, 'which I carry perpetually about with me, in order to study the sentiments – the dauntless magnanimity; the intrepid unyielding independance; the desperate daring, and noble defiance of hardship, in that great personage Satan.' Though he now had 'a little cash', he was fearful for the future. 'Misfortune dodges [*sic*] the path of human life; the poetic mind finds itself miserably deranged in, and unfit for the walks of business; add to all that, thoughtless follies and harebrained whims, like so many Ignes

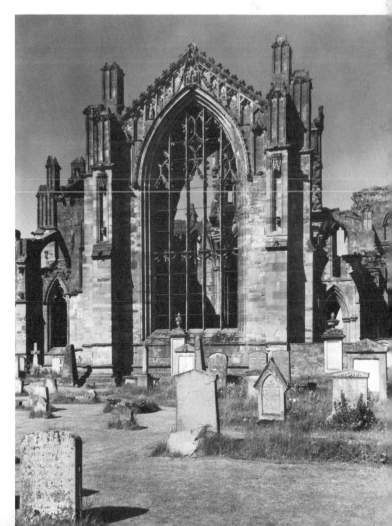

Melrose Abbey. Burns visited what he called 'that far-famed, glorious ruin' on 13 May, a Sunday of pouring rain.

fatui, eternally diverging from the right line of sober discretion, sparkle with step-bewitching blaze in the idly-gazing eyes of the poor heedless Bard, till, pop, "he falls like Lucifer, never to hope again".' Jean Armour's parents, who had been so fiercely opposed to their daughter's marriage to Burns when he was a struggling tenant farmer with dangerous thoughts, were now all servility, but what he called 'their mean, servile compliance' disgusted him and he had no thought at this time of marrying Jean. At the end of June he was off again, on a tour of the Argyllshire Highlands.

At the end of June he wrote to his old Mauchline friend James Smith describing a 'merry party . . . at a Highland gentleman's hospitable mansion' with dancing and singing ('the ladies sung Scotch songs like angels') till three in the morning, when the ladies left and the men stayed up drinking to watch the sun rise over Ben Lomond. Talking, singing, drinking, admiring Highland scenery with congenial companions, flirting with the girls – this was the life, and it was good for his Muse too. But it did not help with his future. In the same letter to Smith he wrote: 'I have yet

Ben Lomond seen from the west. 'I have lately been rambling over by Dumbarton and Inverary, and running a drunken race on the side of Loch Lomond with a wild Highlandman. . . .' (Burns to John Richmond, 7 July 1787)

Jean Armour in old age. She was
born in 1767 and died in 1834.

fixed on nothing with respect to the serious business of life. I am, just as usual, a
rhyming, mason-making, raking, aimless, idle fellow.' But he will have a farm soon,
he continues, although he will never marry.

He was beginning to discover some of the ambiguities of his social position. *Social difficulties*
Though he was made welcome at gentlemen's houses and allowed to talk freely
with their pretty daughters, he was after all a peasant poet and he could not treat these
genteel young ladies as though they were country lasses. More than once he went a
little too far, in words at least, and the young lady, as he once expressed it, 'flew off in
a tangent of female dignity and reserve'. He made many friends among the daughters
of gentlemen, and wrote many poems celebrating their charms, but he had to be
careful. For someone whose 'great constituent elements [were] Pride and Passion',
as he later told Agnes M'Lehose, this meant frustration both psychological and
physical. It is not really surprising that in the intervals of his being lionized by the
nobility and gentry in Edinburgh he had had a physical affair with a servant girl in
the city (she was May Cameron and a letter from her telling him that she was about
to bear his child reached him when he was in Dumfries in June) or that on his
second stay in Edinburgh he should have had a purely physical affair with one
Jenny Clow (who bore him a son) at the very time when he was having a passionate romantic affair with the attractive but respectable and cautious grass widow
Mrs M'Lehose. He was forced to keep his sexual and social contacts in different
compartments.

Jean Armour had borne Burns twins the previous September. Now, on returning
from his West Highland tour in July, he visited mother and children and, for all his

Inverness. Burns and Nicol reached Inverness on Monday, 3 September 1787.

previous resolution, could not refrain from taking up with Jean again, though still holding out against marriage: the result was that Jean again became pregnant and bore him girl twins in March; both of them died soon afterwards. He was back in Edinburgh on 8 August to try and settle with Creech, who had been holding back both on the subscription money and on the hundred guineas. Burns had trouble in getting his money. 'He [Creech] kept me hanging about Edinburgh from the 7th August, 1787, until the 13th April, 1788,' wrote Burns to Dr Moore in January 1789, 'before he would condescend to give me a statement of affairs; nor had I got it even then, but for an angry letter I wrote him, which irritated his pride.' Creech paid Burns the hundred guineas in May 1788 and finally settled with him about the subscription money (from which he probably deducted his own commission) in March 1789, after which Burns withdrew the offensive remarks he had made about him to Moore. Creech brought out a two-volume edition of Burns's poems in 1793, which included some twenty new poems, by far the finest of which was the narra- tive masterpiece *Tam o' Shanter*, but all Burns received for this edition were some complimentary copies.

Highland tour   On 25 August Burns set off from Edinburgh in a chaise on a trip to the High- lands with William Nicol. They went by Linlithgow, Stirling, Crieff, Aberfeldy, Blair Atholl, through Strathspey to Aviemore and then on to Inverness. They then turned east and went by Forres to Elgin, along the southern shore of the Moray Firth to Banff, down the east coast from Peterhead by Aberdeen and Stonehaven to

Montrose (where he spent two days with relatives) and so back to Edinburgh, by way of Dundee, Perth and Kinross, crossing the Firth of Forth at Queensferry. At Blair Atholl he was entertained by the Duke of Atholl for two days and would have yielded to the pressing invitation to stay longer if it had not been for the impatience of the jealous Nicol. Josiah Walker, tutor in the Duke's household, later recorded his impression of Burns:

'His manner was unembarrassed, plain, and firm. He appeared to have complete reliance on his own native good sense for directing his behaviour. He seemed at once to perceive and to appreciate what was due to the company and to himself, and never to forget a proper respect for the separate species of dignity belonging to each. He did not arrogate conversation, but, when led into it, he spoke with ease, propriety, and manliness. He tried to exert his abilities, because he knew it was ability alone gave him a title to be there. The Duke's fine young family attracted much of his admiration; he drank their healths as *honest men and bonnie lasses*, an idea which was much applauded by the company, and with which he has very felicitously

Part of Perth from the North. '. . . Come through the rich harvests and fine hedgerows of the Carse of Gowrie, along the romantic margin of the Grampian Hills, to Perth.' (Burns's Journal, Friday, 14 September 1787)

closed his poem.' [The poem was *The Humble Petition of Bruar Water*, addressed to the Duke of Atholl – or Athole as the old spelling had it – which concludes: 'So may thro' Albion's farthest ken,/To social-flowing glasses,/The grace be – "Athole's honest men,/And Athole's bonnie lasses!"']

Walker gives us one of the few examples we have of Burns's actual conversation:

'As a specimen of his happiness of conception and strength of expression, I will mention a remark which he made on his fellow-traveller, who was walking, at the time, a few paces before us. He was a man of a robust but clumsy person; and while Burns was expressing to me the value he entertained for him, on account of his vigorous talents, although they were clouded at times by coarseness of manners; "in short," he added, "his mind is like his body, he has a confounded strong in-kneed sort of a soul".'

Nicol's in-kneed soul did Burns a real disservice. Angered and offended at Burns's having been asked by the Duke and Duchess of Gordon to stay at Gordon Castle, Fochabers, while he himself was staying at the inn at Fochabers, he insisted on leaving at once, even though the Duke, on hearing of Nicol's presence, cordially

The fourth Duke of Atholl. 'I shall never forget the fine family piece I saw at Blair; the amiable, the truly noble Dutchess with her smiling little seraph in her lap . . .' (Burns to Josiah Walker, 5 September 1787)

Gordon Castle, *c.* 1801.

invited him to stay at the Castle too. But – according to Dr Currie's account, given him by a Fochabers doctor – 'the invitation came too late; the pride of Nicoll [*sic*] was inflamed into a high degree of passion, by the neglect which he had already suffered. He had ordered the horses to be put to the carriage, being determined to proceed on his journey alone. . . . As no explanation nor entreaty could change the purpose of his fellow-traveller, our poet was reduced to the necessity of separating from him entirely, or of instantly proceeding with him on their journey. He chose the last of these alternatives, and seating himself beside Nicoll in the post-chaise, with mortification and regret, he turned his back on Gordon Castle where he had promised himself some happy days.' Burns never saw the Gordons again. But Nicol's dragging Burns away from Blair Atholl was in fact more serious, for among the guests of the Duke and Duchess of Atholl were Robert Graham of Fintry, Commissioner of Excise, the very man Burns needed to cultivate if he was to get a commission in the Excise, while the great Henry Dundas, 'King Harry the Ninth', the most powerful man in Scotland, was expected the next day. A few days longer at Blair Atholl might have made all the difference to Burns's career.

The Duke of Gordon.

This Highland trip was by far the most extensive that Burns had yet taken in Scotland, and he eagerly inspected places known for their historical associations, folk traditions, and physical charms. He had begun his poetic career as a singer of local songs, but his ambition was to be the poet of Scotland. He absorbed local traditions, paid tribute to beauties both human and natural, and cocked his ear continually for local work songs, love songs, and other often fragmentary and half forgotten survivals. He was shortly to begin his great work of re-creating single-handed almost the whole body of Scottish folk song, and it was thanks to his attentive interest in Scottish topography that he was able to anchor song after song in a particular landscape, giving 'a local habitation and a name' to so many of his productions. His songs constitute a litany of celebration of the Scottish countryside. There are no disembodied beauties among Burns's love songs. They all have local names and act out their parts against a local landscape.

In this connection it is worth emphasizing that, for all his fondness for the countryside and his desire to know and celebrate all aspects of Scottish natural scenery, Burns did not have anything approaching that attitude to Nature which came to be called 'Romantic'. Though throughout his childhood and young manhood he lived within sight of the peaks of Arran, he never mentions them in poems or letters. He has a farmer's eye for Nature. Nature for him is where people farm and where young men walk with their girls over fields and by streams when the hard day's agricultural labour is over. For him the 'burnie' 'trots' or 'toddles' down the hillside. He liked the more intimate aspects of Nature; he knew what they meant in terms of daily living. But he also liked visiting historical scenes, and saw with emotion Culloden Moor, where the Jacobite army was bloodily defeated, the ruined cathedral at Elgin, the field of Bannockburn with 'the hole where glorious Bruce set his standard' and at Linlithgow 'the room where the beautiful injured Mary Queen of Scots was born'. He relished, too, seeing the scenes associated with Macbeth, including 'the muir where Shakespeare lays Macbeth's witch meeting'.

Old Leanach cottage on Culloden Moor. 'Come over Culloden muir – reflections on the field of battle . . .' (Burns's Journal, Thursday, 6 September 1787)

South view of Stirling Castle. '. . . Just now, from Stirling Castle, I have seen by the setting sun the glorious prospect of the windings of the Forth through the rich Carse of Stirling . . .' (Burns to Robert Muir, 26 August 1787)

At the same time he cast a professional farmer's eye over the landscape, admiring the 'fine, fruitful, hilly, woody country round Perth' and 'the rich harvests and fine hedge rows' of the Carse of Gowrie.

Burns was back in Edinburgh on 16 September, but on 4 October he was off again, this time with Dr James Adair, to whom he had been introduced by the Reverend George Lawrie. Dr Adair later described the journey for Dr Currie when the latter was writing his biography of Burns. They 'rode by Linlithgow and Carron, to Stirling. . . .' At Stirling the prospects from the castle strongly interested him; on a former visit to it, his national feelings had been powerfully excited by the ruinous and roofless state of the hall in which the Scottish parliaments had frequently been held. From Stirling they went to Harvieston, Clackmannanshire, where they spent some time with the Chalmers family. Mr Chalmers was a gentle-man farmer, his wife was a sister of Gavin Hamilton's stepmother, and their

Margaret (Peggy) Chalmers. 'Personal attractions, madam, you have much above par; wit, understanding, and worth, you possess in the first class . . .' (Burns to Peggy Chalmers, November 1787)

daughter Peggy, whom Burns had met and been much attracted to before, was now the centre of the poet's attentions. He seems to have been really in love with her and to have wanted to marry her. Long afterwards she told the poet Thomas Campbell that Burns had proposed to her and she had rejected him; but they remained friends. It is interesting to speculate what the effect on Burns would have been if he had married as intelligent and accomplished a girl as Peggy Chalmers undoubtedly was. Though he finally married the loving and long-suffering Jean, he knew that she could not provide intellectual companionship for him, and one of the problems of his later life was that his private domestic life was completely cut off from those social circles to which his talents and self-confidence gave him (but not his wife) entry. He was always searching for intellectual companionship, and if it went together with feminine attractiveness, so much the better – and the more dangerous. We shall see later that his association with the intellectually lively and physically attractive Maria Riddell ended in disaster.

While staying at Harvieston Burns visited John Ramsay of Ochtertyre, a scholarly country gentleman who later wrote an important book of reminiscences, and a 'Mrs Bruce, of Clackmannan, a lady above ninety, the lineal descendant of that race which gave the Scottish throne its brightest ornaments'. She and the poet exchanged Jacobite sentiments and together drank the toast 'Awa' Uncos' – that is, 'Away with the strangers' (the House of Hanover). Burns's Jacobitism was, in his own phrase, of the sentimental variety; he was moved by the misfortunes of the House of Stewart but was not seriously in favour of restoring the kind of monarchy which they had represented. It is, on the surface, a paradox that Burns should have been such a fierce democrat and, later, a supporter of the French Revolution, and at the same time could write poems which implied that he was yearning for the Jacobite Pretender to enjoy his own again. But his Jacobitism was pure gesture: his Jacobinism was more serious and was in due course to get him into trouble.

From Harvieston Burns and his friends made excursions to nearby scenes of natural beauty which Dr Adair called 'inferior to none in Scotland, in beauty, sublimity, and romantic interest'. 'I am surprised,' wrote Dr Adair, 'that none of these scenes should have called forth an exertion of Burns's muse. But I doubt if he had much taste for the picturesque. I well remember, that the ladies of Harvieston, who accompanied us on this jaunt, expressed their disappointment at his not expressing in more glowing and fervent language, his impressions of the *Caldron Linn* scene, certainly highly sublime, and somewhat horrible.' Burns had been

Scots wha ha'e. Bruce's address to his troops at Bannockburn. '. . . A kind of Scots Ode, . . . that one might suppose to be the gallant ROYAL SCOT'S address to his heroic followers on that eventful morning.' (Burns to George Thomson, *c.* 30 August 1793)

Edinburgh. Looking up at the Old Town across the North Bridge. The bridge was completed in 1772, linking the Old Town to the site of the New Town by spanning the North Loch valley.

perfectly prepared to act the part of the Heaven-taught ploughman, but he was not going to pretend to a fashionable sensibility which he did not possess.

Burns was back in Edinburgh on 20 October, no longer the great social lion he had been the preceding autumn, for the novelty of the ploughman poet had by now worn off a bit. He was restless and unsettled, disinclined to return to Mossgiel (now being run by his brother Gilbert), not having any other definite course to follow, still hoping for an Excise job. But he had already developed an interest that was to change his life and give him plenty to do. The preceding April he had met in Edinburgh James Johnson, a self-educated lover of Scottish songs who had invented a cheap process for printing music by using stamped pewter plates and who proposed to publish a 'Collection of Scots, English and Irish Songs in two neat 8vo volumes'. The first volume was already in the press when Johnson asked

Burns to help him in collecting Scottish songs for subsequent volumes. No task could have been more congenial to Burns, and by the middle of 1787 he had pretty much taken over the direction of the work and become virtual editor. The title of the work was *The Scots Musical Museum* and between early 1787 and late in 1792 the bulk of Burns's poetic production went into it. In 1792 Burns was approached by George Thomson for similar help in his collection of *Select Scottish Airs*, and Burns responded with equal enthusiasm, supplying Thomson with songs until just before his death. The canalizing of Burns's poetic energies into collecting, reworking, resurrecting and writing songs was in some ways a loss to Scottish poetry, for it turned him away from the satires, verse letters and other forms in which he could perform so brilliantly. His sole narrative poem of any importance, *Tam o' Shanter*, was written by request in 1791 in order to provide an accompaniment for the drawing of Alloway Church in Francis Grose's *Antiquities of Scotland*, and showed what he could do in the vein of quasi-supernatural narrative done with the most deft variations of tone. More commissions of this sort might have been good for him. As it was, the songs captured him, and he devoted himself to them literally almost to his dying day.

Captain Francis Grose. The fat antiquary became a good friend of Burns.

Alloway Church, Ayrshire. Engraving from Francis Grose's *Antiquities of Scotland*.

Burns's desk and other relics. 'Burns cult, forsooth! It has denied his spirit to honour his name. It has denied his poetry to laud his amours. It has preserved his furniture and repelled his message.' (Hugh MacDiarmid, *The Burns Cult*)

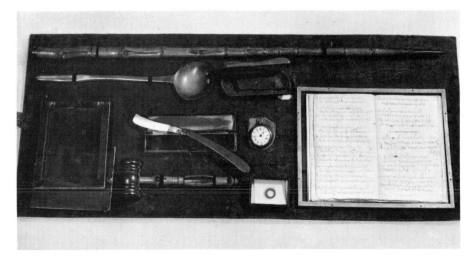

If it was a loss, it was also of course a gain. The fragments of folk song that still floated about Scotland in Burns's day consisted often of little more than a half-remembered chorus. Other songs had been 'improved' by genteel authors into vapid masses of clichés. Burns had a poetic ear uncannily in tune with the folk idiom and also a unique gift for writing verses to a given air. So what he did, not for personal glory but as a contribution to the glory of Scotland, was to re-create virtually the whole corpus of Scottish folk song. He collected fragments and worked them up into complete songs in the spirit of the original. He wrote new songs for airs which had lost their words. He based original songs on debased old models, he wrote alternative sets of words to the same air, he picked up work songs from fisher folk on the Moray Firth or the Fife coast, or from farmers in his native Ayr-shire or from anywhere that he wandered in his journeyings around Scotland, and gave them new form and new life. And always in his songs he was concerned with the cycle of life and love and work as he knew it. He could celebrate both male conviviality and friendship and heterosexual love. He could be tender, passionate, bawdy, satirical, jocular, or plaintive. But always his songs were concerned with the realized moment of experience. His love songs are the antithesis of the love poems of Shelley: there is no philosophizing or Platonic enlargement about them; they concentrate on the experiencing self, indeed on what George Orwell in another connection called the 'unofficial self'. One of the reasons for the world-wide popularity of Burns's songs is that they tell the truth about human feelings without falsification or distortion. Of course, not all his songs are equally successful. But at his best they sound an authentic human voice with extraordinary vibrancy.

There is a limitation in this achievement. Burns's narrowing down of everything to the moment of experience, in such lines as

> *The kirk and state may gae to hell,*
> *And I'll gae to my Anna*

can be excessively limiting in poetic – and indeed in human – scope. But it is also, in Matthew Arnold's famous term, salutary. And even within the limitations the range is remarkable. There is the delighted use of localizing place-names:

> *Willie Wastle dwalls on Tweed,*
> *The spot they ca' it Linkumdoddie.*

One cannot miss the celebration of named places: 'Ye banks and braes o' bonie Doon,' 'Braw, braw lads on Yarrow braes', 'In comin by the brig o' Dye', 'A' the lads o' Thorniebank', 'The Birks of Aberfeldy', 'Elibanks and Elibraes', 'As I cam o'er the Cairney mount', 'The lovely lass o' Inverness', and innumerable others. One can trace Burns's Scottish journeys by the place-names he includes in his songs, for he listened to and picked up local lore about local places. His songs constitute, among other things, a ritual of celebration of Scottish topography. Then there are his Jacobite songs, in which he manages to invest this lost cause with a great range of folk feelings, from the movingly ritualistic *Go fetch to me a pint o' wine* to the rollicking *Charlie he's my Darling*. Work and love can go together in a context of realized country living:

> O, merry hae I been teethin a heckle   flax-comb
>   An' merry hae I been shapin a spoon!
> O, merry hae I been cloutin, a kettle,   patching
>   An' kissin my Katie when a' was done!

But Burns has many other moods of love: there is the benedictory peace of *Ca' the yowes to the knowes*, the relaxed abandon of *It was upon a Lammas night*, the archness of

The Pass of Killiecrankie.

An ye had been whare I hae been,
*   Ye wad na been sae cantie O;*
An ye had seen what I hae seen,
*   I' th' braes o' Killiecrankie O.*

(Killiecrankie)

Dunure Castle and Ailsa Craig.

Duncan fleech'd, and Duncan pray'd;
*   Ha, ha, the wooing o't.*
Meg was deaf as Ailsa Craig,
*   Ha, ha, the wooing o't.*
*   (Duncan Gray)* ▶

The 'glorious river Tweed'.

And we'll tak a cup o' kindness yet
For auld lang syne.

O whistle, and I'll come to ye, my lad, the finely controlled emotion of *Mary Morison*, the pure folk feeling of *O my Luve's like a red, red rose*, the unsentimental tenderness of *John Anderson My Jo*, the protective gentleness of *Oh wert thou in the cauld blast* (written as he lay dying, for Jessie Lewars, the sister of a fellow exciseman, who helped to nurse him), the lilting triumph of the cunningly constructed song he wrote to one of Jean's favourite airs,

> *O luve will venture in where it daur na weel be seen,*

the confident swagger of the song he wrote when he finally married Jean:

> *I hae a wife o' my ain,*
> *I'll partake wi' naebody:*

and the song he wrote for her 'during the honeymoon' as he himself recollected:

> *Of a' the airts the wind can blaw,*   directions
> *I dearly like the West;*
> *For there the bony Lassie lives,*
> *The Lassie I lo'e best.*

Then there were patriotic songs, soldiers' songs, drinking songs (*Willie brew'd a peck o' maut* is one of the best drinking songs in the world), and that simple

90

Title-page to the first volume of *The Scots Musical Museum*. ▶

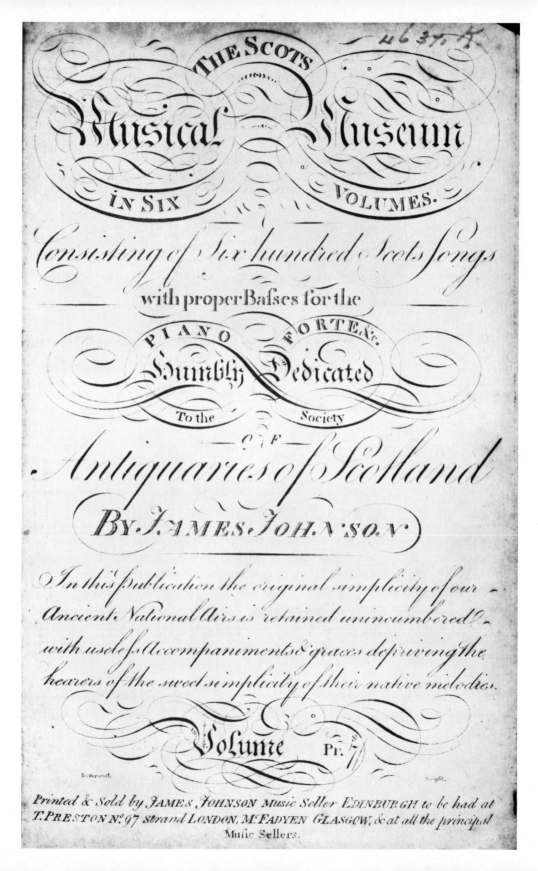

THE SCOTS Musical Museum IN SIX VOLUMES.

Consisting of Six hundred Scots songs

with proper Basses for the

PIANO FORTE &c.

Humbly Dedicated To the Society of

Antiquaries of Scotland

BY JAMES JOHNSON

In this publication the original simplicity of our Ancient National Airs is retained unincumbered with useless Accompaniments & graces depriving the hearers of the sweet simplicity of their native melodies.

Volume Pr. 7/

Printed & Sold by JAMES JOHNSON Music Seller EDINBURGH to be had at T. PRESTON Nº 97 Strand LONDON, McFADYEN GLASGOW, & at all the principal Music Sellers.

Agnes M'Lehose, 'Clarinda'. 'He who sees you as I have done and does not love you, deserves to be damn'd for his stupidity!' (Burns to Clarinda, 4 January 1788)

but moving song of remembered friendship, *Auld Lang Syne,* which Burns never claimed as his own, though the version we know is clearly mostly by him.

Burns would take no money for his great work, nor was he anxious to claim credit for the authorship of many songs which he re-worked in varying degrees. It is in fact impossible to determine exactly what part Burns played in the songs he contributed to Johnson and Thomson. Of course many we know were altogether his own, and many we know were re-fashioned in one way or another. Many were taken down from the performance of a country singer and sometimes mulled over later, to be developed in a variety of ways. Sometimes he just had the tune, which survived as a dance tune with a name but had no longer any words and he wrote new words for the tune; sometimes he wrote words to a dance tune that had never had words. But always he showed the most remarkable skill in fitting words to music and, as his correspondence on these matters with Thomson shows, the most painstaking professional concern to get everything right.

Clarinda   This account of Burns as a song-writer has taken us right up to the end of his life, for from the moment of his starting work to help Johnson he was an avid and unremitting collector and re-fashioner of songs. But of course he was doing other things as well. In December 1787 he met Mrs Agnes M'Lehose, and hence-forth for a considerable time the acquaintance kept him busy. Mrs M'Lehose, or

The much respected Patroness of my early Muse certainly deserved a better return
from me than to let her excellent, her kind letter remain so long
unanswered. — Your elegant epistle, Madam, and your very handsome present, as handsomely delivered, struck me so much, that
I immediately made a private vow to give you a few verses on
the subject; or at least, write you such a Past-sheet as would be
a pennyworth at sixpence. — I have failed in both. — Some
important business respecting my future days, and the miserable dunning and plaguing of Creech, has busied me till
I am good for nothing. — Your criticisms and observations
on the President's Elegy are just. — I am sick of writing
where my bosom is not strongly interested. — Tell me what
you think of the following? there, the <u>bosom</u> was perhaps
a little <u>interested</u>. —

      Clarinda, Mistress of my soul,
        The measur'd time is run!
    The wretch beneath the dreary Pole
        So marks his latest sun. —

Clarinda, Mistress of my soul . . .

'The Young Laird and Edinburgh Katy.' This is the title of a poem by Allan Ramsay in the *Tea-Table Miscellany*; it is the kind of poem by Ramsay that influenced Burns. The illustration shows Edinburgh in Burns's day.

Nancy as her friends called her, had married at seventeen and was now separated from her dissolute and irresponsible husband, to whom she had borne four children, and was living in a flat in Potter Row, Edinburgh, on an annuity together with some assistance from her uncle Lord Craig, a judge of the Court of Session. She consoled herself with religion, and she also had some pretensions to literature. When Burns was being lionized in Edinburgh, she was anxious to meet him, but it was not until 4 December 1787 that they met at a tea party given by her friend Miss Nimmo at the house of Miss Nimmo's brother John Nimmo, an Excise officer. They were at once mutually attracted, and Nancy invited Burns to call on her the following Thursday. But Burns having accepted found that he could not manage to come on that day, and wrote, enclosing a poetic *bagatelle*, proposing the following Saturday. An injury to his knee caused by a fall from a coach prevented him from keeping this second appointment. Confined to his room, Burns started an epistolary affair with Nancy, a curious hothouse correspondence in which he was 'Sylvander' and she was 'Clarinda' and they both advanced and retreated from actual declarations of love in a highly sentimental verbal ballet which represented a remarkable *tour de force* on Burns's part. The relationship continued when Burns was well enough to visit her in early January and the correspondence and the visits went on, rising to a peak in the middle of February. What exactly happened at Potter Row we can only surmise, but it seems clear that

Clarinda had more than once to summon all her religion to her aid to resist the physical advances of Sylvander. They probably took it out in verbal play, sometimes of the most extravagant kind, while Burns satisfied his more physical needs with less respectable Edinburgh girls. Clarinda's discovery of this fact, together with Burns's eventual acknowledgement of Jean as his wife, led to a rupture in the relationship. The Clarinda-Sylvander affair is an extraordinary chapter in Burns's emotional history. It produced a handful of love songs, most of them fairly frigid exercises in neo-classic idiom, and one great final song of parting, written in 1791 after Clarinda had more or less forgiven Burns and was preparing to rejoin her husband in the West Indies, *Ae fond kiss, and then we sever*, with its haunting fourth stanza:

> *Had we never lov'd sae kindly,*
> *Had we never lov'd sae blindly!*
> *Never met – or never parted,*
> *We had ne'er been broken-hearted.*

Meanwhile Burns was continuing with his efforts to get a commission in the Excise, writing both to Graham of Fintry and to the Earl of Glencairn asking for their aid. He left Edinburgh on 18 February 1788 and on 23 February was writing to Clarinda from Mossgiel that he had seen 'a certain woman' – Jean Armour – and 'I am disgusted with her; I cannot endure her! I, while my heart smote me for the prophanity, tried to compare her with my Clarinda: 'twas setting the expiring glimmer of a farthing taper beside the cloudless glory of the meridian sun'. He added that 'I have done with her, and she with me'. On 2 March he wrote to Clarinda that he now thought well of the 'farming scheme' offered by Patrick

Poem to Mr Graham of Fintry, 'one of the worthiest and most accomplished gentlemen, not only of this Country, but I will dare to say it, of this Age.' (Burns to Mrs Dunlop, 2 August 1788)

Miller. The next day he wrote from Mauchline to his friend Robert Ainslie a letter which Burns's stoutest champions find it difficult to explain or forgive:

'I have been through sore tribulation, and under much buffeting of the Wicked One, since I came to this country. Jean I found banished like a martyr – forlorn, destitute, and friendless; all for the good old cause [she was pregnant again as a result of Burns's association with her the previous summer, and actually bore twins on the very day Burns was writing]: I have reconciled her to her fate: I have reconciled her to her mother: I have taken her a room: I have taken her to my arms: I have given her a mahogany bed: I have given her a guinea; and I have f——d her till she rejoiced with joy unspeakable and full of glory. But – as I always am on every occasion – I have been prudent and cautious to an astounding degree; I swore her, privately and solemnly, never to attempt any claim on me as a husband, even though anybody should persuade her she had such a claim, which she has not, neither during my life, nor after my death. . . .'

It is difficult to know what to make of this letter. Jean was on the point of bearing twins, and it is hard to believe that Burns was telling the truth. It has been suggested that Burns had already decided to marry Jean and wrote as he did to Mrs M'Lehose and to Ainslie to throw them off the scent until after he had acknowledged the marriage and received the Excise instructions which he now confidently hoped for; Mrs M'Lehose could have made trouble for him in Edinburgh if she had suspected his insincerity in his protestations to her. At any rate on 7 March he was hinting to Richard Brown that he regarded himself as Jean's husband and late in April he acknowledged her as his wife (such an acknowledgement was enough in Scots law to constitute a retrospective legal marriage), writing to James Smith on 28 April: 'there is, you must know, a certain clean-limbed, handsome, bewitching young hussy of your acquaintance, to whom I have lately and privately given a matrimonial title to my corpus. . . . I hate to presage ill-luck; and as my girl has been *doubly* kinder to me than even the best of women usually are to their partners of our sex, in similar circumstances, I reckon on twelve times a brace of children against I celebrate my twelfth wedding-day. . . .' On the same day he wrote to Mrs Dunlop, 'I commence farmer at Whitsunday' and that he had been offered a course of instruction in 'the Excise business' which on completion would entitle him to a commission in the Excise 'on my simple petition'. It was something in reserve if farming at Ellisland – such was the name of the Dumfriesshire farm he leased from Miller – should prove unsuccessful. He received his Excise instructions in April and May, and settled at Ellisland on 11 June. On 14 July his Excise commission was issued; this did not guarantee him a job in the Excise service, but certified his eligibility for one. It was actually over a year before he began duty as an Excise officer.

Mauchline (Machlin) Castle in 1789. It was then the property of Gavin Hamilton.

The farm of Ellisland lies six and a half miles north-west of Dumfries on the west bank of the River Nith. When Burns moved there in June 1788 there was no farmhouse to which he could bring his wife and only surviving child and he had to arrange to have one built while he left his family at Mauchline. The building proved a slow business. Meanwhile, Burns worked busily on the farm, Jean joining him in December (in temporary accommodation) to look after the dairy. He reaped his first harvest that autumn. It was late spring or early summer before they were settled in the new farmhouse.

The lease on Ellisland is in existence. It provided that Patrick Miller should advance Burns three hundred pounds on condition that he built a dwelling house, did the necessary enclosing, and carried out such improvements on the farm as Burns 'shall deem most expedient'. Burns's rent was seventy pounds yearly, 'but to be restricted to the first three years and crops to fifty pounds'. It was not a good bargain. The land was stony and exhausted, unfertilized and undrained. Many years after Burns's death, Patrick Miller admitted this. 'When I purchased this estate,' he wrote in September 1810, 'about twenty five years ago, I had not seen it. *It was in the most miserable state of exhaustion*, and all the tenants in poverty. Judge of the first when I inform you, that oats ready to be cut were sold at 25s. per acre upon the holm-grounds. *When I went to view my purchase, I was so much disgusted for eight or ten days, that I then meant never to return to this county.*' Burns, who was a

97

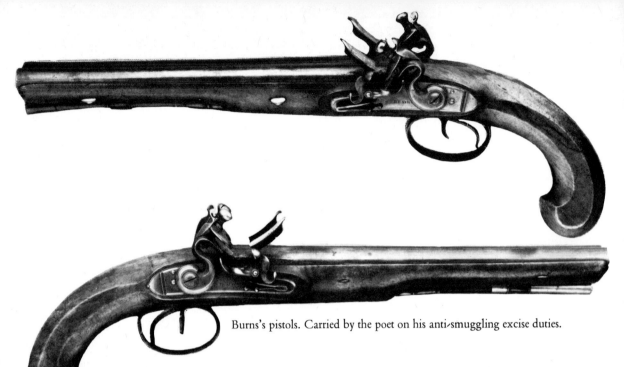

Burns's pistols. Carried by the poet on his anti-smuggling excise duties.

Burns as exciseman

conscientious farmer, could not make a go of it either in arable farming or in dairy farming. 'My farm is a ruinous bargain, & would ruin me to abide by it', he wrote to Mrs Dunlop in March 1790. He had finally got an Excise appointment the previous September, being put in charge of the 'Dumfries first Itinerary' at a salary of fifty pounds a year, and he was combining his Excise duties (which involved watching for smuggling and seeing that weights and measures conformed to the legal standard) with farming. This meant much riding about, over bad roads and in all sorts of weather. Inevitably, the emphasis at the farm turned more to the dairy side, which Jean could supervise. 'The Excise,' Burns continued in his letter to Mrs Dunlop, 'notwithstanding all my objections to it, pleases me tolerably well; it is indeed my sole dependance. – At Martinmass 1791, my rent rises 20 £ per Annum, & *then*, I am, on the maturest deliberation, determined to give it up; & still, even *then*, I shall think myself well quit, if I am no more than a hundred pounds out of Pocket. – So much for Farming! Would to God I had never engaged in it!' On 10 September 1791 Burns signed a formal renunciation of the Ellisland lease and the following November moved with his family to Dumfries, where he lived until his death on 21 July 1796.

Burns was a good Exciseman, though it was ironical that a poet who had sung the praises of 'Scotch drink' so fervently should now be spending much of his time searching for illicit liquor and 'looking down auld wives' barrels', as he put it. In July 1790 his salary was increased to seventy-five pounds a year, on his promotion to the Dumfries '3rd, or Tobacco, Division', which involved covering less distances so that he could dispense with his horse and go on foot. In February 1792 Burns led a boarding party on the grounded schooner *Rosamond*, engaged in smuggling in the Solway Firth, and was subsequently active in guarding, repairing and refloating the ship and in organizing the sale of its confiscated cargo. There is a story, which modern scholarship finds reason to believe to be true, that Burns himself purchased three guns from the *Rosamond* and sent them to France to show his sympathy with the revolutionary government there. True or not, the story accurately reflects Burns's sympathies with the French Revolution which produced an official inquiry into his loyalty in December 1792 and a humiliating recantation on Burns's part. With the declaration of war by France against Britain on 1 February 1793 Burns's patriotism overcame his enthusiasm for the French Revolution, already much diminished (as he told Graham of Fintry in a long letter of explanation and excuse) when France showed 'her old avidity for conquest, in annexing Savoy, &c. to her dominions, & invading the rights of Holland'.

What sort of life did Burns lead at Ellisland and then at Dumfries in his last eight years? The answer to this question sums up all the difficulties, frustrations, ambiguities and paradoxes of Burns's life. He had married his Jean out of genuine affection and good nature. She loved him, she had given herself to him unconditionally, and when it came to the crunch he could not bring himself to reject her. She devoted her life to him, cheerfully and uncensoriously: when he fathered a daughter on Anna Park (for whom he wrote the love song, *Yestreen, I had a pint o' wine*), niece of the landlady of the Globe Inn in Dumfries, she brought up the

Last years

The Wreckers. Detail of a painting by George Morland.

Window pane from the Globe Inn. Burns's habit of inscribing radical sentiments in odd places sometimes got him into trouble.

◀ Burns's House, Dumfries. Situated in what was then Mill Street, now Burns Street, the house has been preserved as a museum. Burns rented it for £8 per annum from Captain John Hamilton of Allershaw.

The Globe Inn. The entrance today is through a 'close' at 56 High Street. In Burns's day there was vacant ground in front and to the right of the building. The poet's favourite seat was to the right of the fireplace, and his chair is still kept there.

Design for a stage set for the Dumfries Theatre, made at the request of Burns. Drawing by Alexander Nasmyth, c. 1795.

101

Maria Riddell.
'Farewell, thou first of
Friends, & most
accomplished of
Women; even with all
thy little caprices!!!'
(Conclusion of letter
from Burns to Maria,
April 1793)

child with her own, calmly observing that 'Oor Rab should hae had twa wives'.
She herself bore him in all nine children, the last posthumously on the day of Burns's
funeral. Yet, though she could sing his songs, she could not share his literary and
intellectual interests and could not provide him with the kind of conversation
which he needed and at which he excelled. Burns made friends with the local
gentry, attended their parties and engaged in witty talk with them, while his wife
stayed at home. The class situation was in fact intolerable. Burns was allowed –
within limits – to transcend his class because of his genius. This involved him
in social relationships wholly separated from his domestic life and sometimes
dangerously balanced between equality and (on his hosts' part) condescension. He
continued to collect and re-fashion and create songs, and to write poems, trivial and
serious, complimentary, celebratory, convivial, epigrammatic and satirical, and
to read widely in seventeenth- and eighteenth-century literature. He corresponded
eagerly with Thomson about Scottish songs. But he was not grounded in a way of
life that provided him with a proper emotional security. He remained a divided
personality.

Some of the problems of his way of life and thought are reflected in his correspondence with George Thomson, whose genteel view of Scottish songs led him to
suggest alterations and emasculations that Burns kept resisting with patient argument. More revealing is his relationship with the Riddell family. Robert Riddell, a

The Hermitage, Friar's Carse, built by Captain Robert Riddell on his beautiful estate on the river Nith. Burns used to go there to sit and meditate.

retired army captain, lived on the Glenriddell estate at Friars' Carse, less than a mile north of Ellisland. He interested himself in antiquarian matters and in Scots song, and composed some song tunes for which Burns wrote the words. Riddell and Burns became good friends soon after Burns settled at Ellisland, and Burns was given the key to a 'hermitage' on the Riddell estate. On 16 October 1789, there took place a celebrated bacchanalian contest which Burns described in his poem *The Whistle*. It was for Riddell that Burns prepared an interleaved copy of *The Scots Musical Museum* with copious notes in his own hand, and he also transcribed for him two manuscript books (together known as the Glenriddell MSS.) of his selected poems and letters. Through Riddell Burns got to know his younger brother Walter and Walter's vivacious and attractive young wife Maria. Burns and Maria Riddell exchanged spirited letters, and there was clearly an attraction between them. But at the end of December 1793, when Maria's husband was in the West Indies, an incident occurred at Friars' Carse which shattered the friendship between Burns and Maria and demonstrated the precariousness of Burns's social position.

What exactly occurred will never be known for certain, but it appears that at a party at which all the men had been drinking heavily it was proposed that the men act out the 'Rape of the Sabines' and Burns was egged on to act his part vigorously. He apparently acted it out all too vigorously, probably not on Maria but on Robert

'Mixtures not always salutary . . .'. A group of men drinking, including Burns. Drawing by Thomas Stothard.

Riddell's wife Elizabeth, and in doing so gave great offence to the whole Riddell family. At any rate, Maria, either out of loyalty to the Riddells or because she was genuinely outraged (it may be that she rather than Elizabeth was Burns's victim – the details are far from clear), joined in the subsequent ostracizing of Burns. Burns was furious, and his affectionate admiration for Maria turned to furious anger, especially after his agonized apology (in a letter conjecturally addressed to Mrs Robert Riddell) was ignored. His pride was deeply hurt, and he took it out on Maria in offensive verse lampoons. They were not reconciled until shortly before Burns's death.

The most significant point about this incident was that if Burns had been of the same social class as the Riddells the whole thing would have been passed off as a drunken jest. This was a hard-drinking age, and, as innumerable contemporary accounts make clear, Scottish gentlemen frequently went to bed night after night dead drunk. The most respected and respectable people in the country, the judges on the bench and the *literati* at their parties, regularly consumed vast amounts of alcohol. Burns was not a hard drinker by the standards of his day. But he did not have a good head for liquor, and when he did drink he was liable to lose control. This could be highly dangerous when he was in the process of walking the social tight-rope that was his inevitable lot when attending parties at gentlemen's houses. When we remember the 'Pride and Passion' that were so prominent in his social make-up, we can only be surprised that Burns did not become involved in more social catastrophes than he actually suffered.

Burns certainly drank a good deal, and was sometimes drunk. But the censoriousness with which this was discussed, especially immediately after his death, had social rather than moral causes. It did not become a peasant poet who was patronized by the gentry to compete with the gentry in their drinking habits. A further point to bear in mind is that drink had nothing to do with Burns's early death from rheumatic endocarditis. Indeed, one medical authority has argued that he would have died even sooner if he had never touched alcohol.

Burns's extravagant sexual life is part of the same pattern of social ambiguity and confusion. He had to separate intellectual admiration, romantic passion, and sexual activity. He cherished throughout his life a domestic ideal of 'a happy

Letter from Burns to his friend John M'Murdo, 1792.

fireside clime, wi' weans and wife', and he enjoyed domesticity. But clearly his domesticity with Jean and her children was not enough for him. Of course, it must be added that Burns was extremely highly sexed, and also that he was a great lover of bawdy. His collection of bawdy songs made for his private friends (known as *The Merry Muses of Caledonia*) is sufficient testimony to this. But his relish of bawdy was frank and Rabelaisian, never prurient and suggestive. Further, as has already been observed, he linked sexual pleasure with joy in parenthood in a way that is difficult if not impossible to parallel among poetic libertines (Byron, for example).

Burns and politics   If drink and sex presented one problem for Burns in the confused social context in which he moved, politics presented another. Beside the quarrel with Maria Riddel we can set Burns's break with Mrs Dunlop, with whom he had corresponded assiduously ever since their first acquaintance in 1786 and who played an almost maternal role with respect to him. Mrs Dunlop did not really understand or appreciate the livelier moods of Burns's muse, but this did not prevent him from confiding in her both his poetic ambitions and his general views of life. But politics were more dangerous. In January 1795 Burns, continuing a long letter to Mrs

Execution of Louis XVI, 26 January 1793.

Dr John Moore (1729–1802), surgeon and novelist. Mrs Dunlop sent him a copy of the Kilmarnock edition of Burns's poems in 1786 and this caused Moore to ask that Burns should send him some account of his life. The result was Burns's long autobiographical letter to Moore of August 1787 – a key document for students of Burns's life and character.

Dunlop that he had started on 20 December, attacked a recent publication on France by Dr Moore. 'I cannot approve of the honest Doctor's whining over the deserved fate of a certain pair of Personages', he wrote. 'What is there in the delivering over a perjured Blockhead & an unprincipled Prostitute to the hands of the hangman, that it should arrest for a moment, attention, in an eventful hour, when, as my friend Roscoe in Liverpool gloriously expresses it –

> *"When the welfare of Millions is hung in the scale*
> *And the balance yet trembles with fate!"'*

Such a reference to the execution of Louis XVI and Marie Antoinette was bound to be offensive to the conservative Mrs Dunlop even if two of her daughters had not been married to French royalist refugees. She broke with Burns, and ignored his subsequent letters. He wrote movingly to ask what 'sin of ignorance' he had 'committed against so highly valued a friend'. But it was only when he was literally on his death-bed that she relented, and a friendly message from her was almost the last line he read.

Burns's political activities also concerned themselves with events nearer home. He wrote a letter to William Pitt, in his most eloquent English rhetorical style, on

107

behalf of the Scottish distilleries suffering from 'a most partial tax laid on by the House of Commons, to favour a few opulent English Distillers': this appeared in the *Edinburgh Evening Courant* of 9 February 1789, signed 'JOHN BARLEY-CORN – Praeses'. In the previous November he had written to the same newspaper expressing with reasoned clarity his considered views of Jacobitism, the English Revolution of 1688 and the American Revolution of 1776. He wrote election ballads in the parliamentary contests of 1790 and 1795, dealing with local issues and personalities with great satirical vigour. He contributed more general political verse satires to the London *Morning Star*, though he declined its editor's invitation to be a regular contributor. But he let nothing interfere with his continued work on Scottish song.

Dumfries   Dumfries, though not possessing the best climate for someone with Burns's rheumatic complaint, was a lively and interesting town of which he had been made an honorary burgess in June 1787. He cashed in on this honour in 1793 by applying successfully to have his children educated in the burgh school without paying 'the

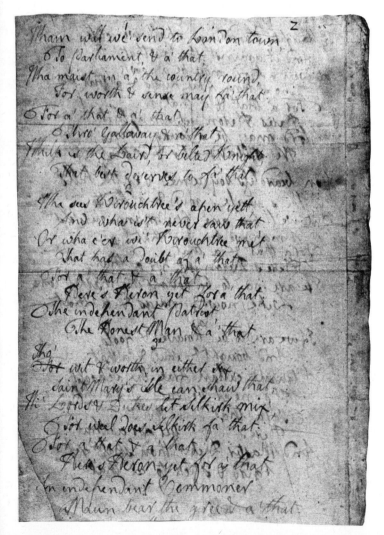

An election ballad for Patrick Heron. Heron stood for Parliament as Whig candidate for the Stewartry of Kirkudbright, and Burns helped him by writing satirical ballads against his opponents.

John Syme (1755–1831), who was appointed Distributor of Stamps in Dumfries in 1791. He lived in a villa at Ryedale and Burns often dined with him there.

Letter from Burns to the Lord Provost, Bailies and Town Council of Dumfries, March 1793.

high School-fees which a Stranger pays'. He made new friends in Dumfries, including Dr William Maxwell, who had travelled in France during the Revolution and had returned ardent in its support; John Syme, with whom Burns made a tour of Galloway in June 1794; Alexander Findlater, Supervisor of the Dumfries Excise District; John Lewars, a fellow exciseman whose sister Jessie helped to nurse Burns in his last illness; and James Gray, a Dumfries school teacher, who wrote an attractive account of a visit to Burns's home when he found the poet reading and explaining to his children 'the English poets from Shakespeare to Gray'. Though he sometimes broke out into drinking bouts, Burns's life at Dumfries was far from being a round of dissipation. He had regular moods of deep depression (associated with his illness) and was often very unwell. In spite of his brush with his superiors at the Excise over his support for the French Revolution (an incident which left a permanent mark on him, for he was now becoming increasingly worried about his ability to support his family and to leave them decently off when he died), he enjoyed their respect and good will. There was never any criticism of his efficiency as an Excise officer.

109

George Thomson. His *Select Collection of Original Scotish* [sic] *Airs* was planned as a much more elegant work than Johnson's *Scots Musical Museum*. His gentility and conventionality caused Burns much trouble, and since all but the first number of his work appeared after Burns's death, he freely disregarded Burns's instructions about particular songs and their settings.

It was of course preposterous that Burns produced all the songs for Johnson and Thomson for nothing, but in a sense it was his own fault, for his pride refused to allow him to discuss financial terms. It was in September 1792 that George Thomson wrote to Burns about his plan to bring out a collection of 'the most favourite of our national melodies' and asked Burns's help in providing words. What he wanted was a few genteel and sentimental lyrics, and he must have been surprised at Burns's excited response. 'As the request you make to me,' Burns replied on 16 September, 'will positively add to my enjoyments in complying with it, I shall enter into your undertaking with all the small portion of abilities I have, strained to their utmost exertion by the impulse of Enthusiasm. – Only, don't hurry me.' He went on to say, 'if you are for *English* verses, there is, on my part, an end of the matter'. He insisted on 'at least a sprinkling of our native tongue'. He goes on to give examples of what he means, and the whole letter breathes high excitement. He concludes:

'As to any remuneration, you may think my Songs either *above*, or *below* price; for they shall absolutely be the one or the other. – In the honest enthusiasm with which I embark in your undertaking, to talk of money, wages, fee, hire, &c. would be downright Sodomy of Soul! – A proof of each of the Songs that I com⁄ pose or amend, I shall receive as a favor. – In the rustic phrase of the Season, "Gude speed the wark!"'

Thomson's suggestion, like that of Johnson before him, touched something in Burns that he himself could hardly control. Neither editor could have anticipated the blaze of excitement with which Burns set about fulfilling – and far more than fulfilling – his commission. It was this high idealistic motive that led him to refuse to take money for the work. It was an unrealistic and, as it turned out, unfortunate

Jean Armour Burns with her granddaughter, Sarah.

The room where Burns died.

gesture, as Burns's last letter to Thomson, less than a fortnight before his death, makes clear:

'After all my boasted independance, curst necessity compels me to implore you for five pounds. – A cruel scoundrel of a Haberdasher to whom I owe an account, taking it into his head that I am dying, has commenced a process, & will infallibly put me into jail. – Do, for God's sake, send me that sum, & that by return of post. – Forgive me this earnestness, but the horrors of a jail have made me half distracted. . . .'

He solemnly promises to repay Thomson 'with five pounds' worth of the neatest song-genius you have seen'. Meanwhile, he is still engaged with songs. 'I tryed my hand on Rothiemurche this morning', he tells Thomson. The man was literally dying, yet he enclosed his latest song, *Fairest maid on Devon banks* to the tune of 'Rothiemurche's Rant'.

He was sent to Brow, on the Solway Firth, in the belief that sea-bathing might cure him, and in the intervals of engaging in this killing activity he wrote to Thomson about his songs, though he could not help exclaiming at one point, 'Alas! is this a time for me to woo the Muses?' He returned from Brow on 18 July and found his wife expecting a baby imminently. He wrote at once to his father-in-law James Armour asking him to send Mrs Armour to Dumfries immediately. 'My wife is hourly expecting to be put to bed. Good God! what a situation for her to be in, poor girl, without a friend!' He adds that his friends are trying to persuade him that he is better, but he feels so weak that he thinks the disorder will prove fatal to him. It was his last letter: he died three days later, on 21 July. He had been sinking steadily for six months of an ailment that was then incurable. Modern medical opinion has diagnosed rheumatic fever with perhaps bacterial endocarditis present terminally. Today, with more rapid recognition of the symptoms, treatment would be with antibiotics and perhaps also with cortisone. The modern diagnosis is pretty definite, for Burns describes his symptoms frequently in his letters. It is certainly clear that neither venereal disease nor alcoholism had anything to do with Burns's death; there is not the slightest evidence that he ever suffered from either and much positive evidence that he did not.

Burns's achievement was astonishing. At a time when Scottish culture was split into a genteel anglicizing stream (by far the most influential), a half-antiquarian, half-debased-vernacular stream, and a current of fragmented and often corrupted folk song, Burns was able to weld together elements from all three to produce a body of poetry which has no equal anywhere for vigour, individuality and powerful human appeal. A peasant thrown into genteel society, he was surrounded by advice and even pressure to conform to the canons of taste and style then prevailing among the leaders of literary fashion. He sometimes yielded to this pressure, in duty poems and 'occasional' pieces of various kinds, and there is evidence that in some moods he enjoyed writing fashionable verse spontaneously; but the remarkable thing is that for the most part he remained true to his own genius, which was fully formed before he encountered the Edinburgh gentry. It is not the moralizing, sententious and rhetorical Burns that we appreciate today: it is the brilliant satirical poet, the master of the verse letter, the poet of friendship and of sexual love, the master (though only on one occasion) of perfectly paced verse narrative, and the greatest song-writer in any language. Yet he was not a pioneer. He did not, as later literary historians were to imagine, foreshadow the Romantic movement, in spite of the fact that the idea of a peasant poet writing of the ordinary experiences of humble life was to appeal to Wordsworth and other Romantics. His achievement marked the end, not the beginning, of a long tradition. He was the heir of the medieval Scottish poets Henryson and Dunbar in his controlled tenderness and in the strength and colour of his imagery; he was the heir of the anonymous Scottish balladists in his deep sense of the folk tradition and his ability to link emotion with the ordinary round of daily living in an agricultural society; he was the heir of the Scottish Court poets of the seventeenth century in the skill with which he shaped a stanza; he was the heir of Robert Fergusson in his reconstructing of a Scottish poetic idiom out of a mixture of colloquial and literary language. His poetry marked, as Scotland's last Lord Chancellor said of Scotland's last Parliament, 'the end of an auld sang'. He was the last poet to be able to handle a Scottish poetic tradition until the Scottish poetic renaissance started by Hugh MacDiarmid in our own century.

Burns was a convivial man, and would not have objected to the annual social gatherings with which his birthday is celebrated. But he would have objected to

Burns's monument,
Kilmarnock, which
was unveiled on
9 August 1879.

some of the things said about him in the speeches delivered on those occasions. And he would have been disconcerted to know the influence he was to have in the nineteenth century. Burns was writing just when the Industrial Revolution was about to change the face of much of Lowland Scotland. Looking back from the nineteenth century with nostalgia for an idealized rural Scotland, later poets and critics saw Burns as the sentimentalizing celebrator of Scottish peasant life, and they wrote their couthie and pawkie dialect poems in the fond belief that they were perpetuating the Burns tradition. Burns's influence on Scottish poetry has not been good, and it is understandable that the modern movement began with the cry 'Back to Dunbar!' But it is not Burns's fault if he has been misunderstood and misused. The fault lies with the increasing decay of the Scots language that went on in the nineteenth century side by side with the growth of a heavy nostalgia as the primary Scottish national emotion.

The remarkable thing about Burns is that he survived at all as a poet of integrity when we consider the currents by which he was buffeted. The rationalizing optimism of the Scottish Enlightenment, the romantic appeal of the Jacobite tradition, the democratic appeal of the French Revolution all pulled at him, as did the folk tradition he learned from the old maid of his mother, the Scottish patriotism he first acquired from reading a modernized version of Blind Harry's *Wallace*, and

Bronze statue of Burns, Irvine. It was unveiled by Alfred Austin, poet laureate, on 18 July 1896. ▶

the fragments of old Scottish folk song that were still floating about the countryside. What was an Ayrshire peasant to make of all this? That he blended these ingredients in his own way is a remarkable tribute to his strength of mind. He knew what he wanted to do, and he did it. He started off as the celebrator of the events and the physical features of his native Ayrshire, reached out to become the poet of Scotland, and in doing so became (as the extraordinary number of translations of his poems and songs throughout the world testifies) the poet of mankind in a way that no other poet can claim to be.

Burns was probably the least transcendental poet who ever lived. His imagination did not soar to the heavens. He looked down at earth and around him, at eye-level, at his fellow-men. He told the truth about man – and woman – at work and at play and in love – and in lust – with a special kind of clarity and integrity. Literary criticism, especially modern criticism, finds it hard to come to terms with him, for the most fashionable critical tools seem inappropriate in discussing his poetry. It is not that Burns does not possess high technical skill, for both the language and the structure of his best poetry will repay the closest analysis. The reason is rather that he speaks to man's 'unofficial self' in a way that is both exciting and disturbing. His is a kind of literature that seems to by-pass literature, as it were. These are not so much poems on the page as Robert Burns speaking or singing to us in a voice highly trained and cunningly modulated but at the same time recognizably, deeply, uncomfortably and movingly human.

Burial-place of Robert Burns. Burns was given a military funeral by the Gentleman Volunteers of Dumfries. He was buried in the north-east corner of St Michael's churchyard, Dumfries, but in September 1815 his body was transferred to the mausoleum that had been erected by public subscription in the south-east corner of the churchyard.

SELECT BIBLIOGRAPHY

David Daiches, *Robert Burns*, revised edition (London and New York 1966)

Hans Hecht, *Robert Burns*, translated by Jane Lymburn, 2nd revised edition (London 1950)

De Lancey Ferguson (ed.), *The Letters of Robert Burns*, 2 vols (Oxford 1931)

De Lancey Ferguson, *Pride and Passion: Robert Burns 1759–1796* (New York 1939)

Maurice Lindsay, *The Burns Encyclopedia*, 2nd revised edition (London 1970)

F. B. Snyder, *The Life of Robert Burns* (New York 1932)

CHRONOLOGY

1759 25 January: Robert Burns born at Alloway, eldest son of William Burnes and his wife Agnes Broun

1765 Robert and his brother Gilbert sent to John Murdoch's school, Alloway Miln

1766 William Burnes rents Mount Oliphant farm

1773 Burns writes his first song, *Handsome Nell*, for Nellie Kirkpatrick

1775 Burns attends Hugh Roger's school at Kirkoswald

1777 Whitsun: the family moves to Lochlie

1780 The Tarbolton Bachelors' Club organized by Burns

1781 William Burnes's dispute with his landlord, David M'Lure, begins. Burns courts Alison Begbie. Becomes a freemason. Summer: goes to Irvine to learn flax-dressing

1783 Starts his first Commonplace Book

1784 William Burnes wins his case in the Court of Session but dies 13 February. The family moves to Mossgiel

1785 Burns composes his first satires and *The Jolly Beggars*. Meets Jean Armour

1786 3 April: 'Proposals' for the Kilmarnock Poems sent to press. James Armour rejects Burns as a son-in-law and issues a writ against him. 31 July: Kilmarnock Poems published. 3 September: Jean Armour bears twins, Robert and Jean. 29 November: Burns arrives in Edinburgh. 14 December: William Creech issues subscription bills for Edinburgh edition of Poems

1787 21 April: Edinburgh Poems published. Burns sells his copyright for 100 guineas. 5 May–1 June: tour of Border country. Late June: tour of West Highlands as far as Inveraray. 25 August–16 September: Highland tour with William Nicol. 4–20 October: tour of Stirlingshire. Vol. 1 of *Scots Musical Museum* published in May, Burns starts work for this collection in November. 4 December: meets Agnes M'Lehose. *Clarinda* correspondence begins

1788 23 February: returns to Mauchline. March: Vol. 2 of *Scots Musical Museum* published. April: acknowledges Jean Armour as his wife and commences Excise instruction at Mauchline. 11 June: moves to Ellisland

1789 16 February: to Edinburgh to close accounts with Creech. 1 September: begins duty as Excise Officer

1790 February: Vol. 3 of *Scots Musical Museum* published

1791 April: 'Tam o' Shanter' published in Grose's *Antiquities of Scotland* and in March edition of *Edinburgh Magazine*. 10 September: signs formal renunciation of Ellisland lease and, 11 November, moves to Dumfries

1792 February: Burns promoted to Dumfries Port Division and organizes capture of schooner *Rosamond*. August: Vol. 4 of *Scots Musical Museum* published. 16 September: starts work for Thomson's *Select Collection*

1793 Official inquiry into Burns's loyalty. 5 January: makes his defence to Graham of Fintry. February: 2nd Edinburgh edition of Poems published. June: 1st Number of Thomson's *Select Collection* published. About 30 July–2 August: first tour of Galloway with Syme

1794 12 January: quarrel with Maria Riddell. About 25 June: second tour of Galloway with Syme. About 22 December: appointed Acting Supervisor at Dumfries

1795 February: reconciliation with Maria Riddell. December: taken ill with rheumatic fever

1796 3 July: to the Brow Well on Solway Firth for sea-bathing cure which fails. 18 July: return to Dumfries where he dies 21 July. 25 July: funeral takes place at St Michael's, Dumfries and Jean bears his ninth child, Maxwell. December: Vol. 5 of *Scots Musical Museum* published

LIST OF ILLUSTRATIONS

19 Lochlie Farm; sepia drawing attributed to William Bartlett, *c.* 1840. National Gallery of Scotland, Edinburgh, Department of Prints and Drawings. Photo: National Galleries of Scotland

20 Tarbolton; engraving by J. C. Armytage after William Bartlett. From A. Cunningham: *Pictures and Portraits of the Life and Land of Robert Burns*, 1840. British Museum

Mauchline; engraving by H. Adlard after William Bartlett. From A. Cunningham: *Pictures and Portraits of the Life and Land of Robert Burns*, 1840. British Museum

22 Trade Card for the Edinburgh Linen Hall; engraving by John Runciman, late eighteenth century. Bodleian Library, Oxford, Gough Map Collection 38 (52). Photo: Oxford University Press

23 'The Common Method of Beetling, Scutching and Hackling the Flax'; aquatint by William Hincks, 1791. Victoria and Albert Museum, London, Print Room. Photo: Eileen Tweedy

24 First page of the service copy petition by David M'Lure against William Burnes alleging that William Burnes owed him over £500; manuscript, 17 May 1783. Trustees of the Burns Monument, Alloway

25 William Burnes's grave, Alloway churchyard. Photo: Scottish Tourist Board

26 Robert Burns and Gavin Hamilton at Nanse Tinnock's; engraving by J. Rogers. From A. Cunningham: *Pictures and Portraits of the Life and Land of Robert Burns,* 1840. British Museum

27 Gilbert Burns; silhouette from *Catalogue of the Burns Exhibition*, 1896. Scottish National Portrait Gallery, Edinburgh. Photo: National Galleries of Scotland

Robert Burns; silhouette by (?)Samuel Houghton of Dumfries, *c.* 1795. Trustees of the Burns Monument, Alloway

28 Mossgiel Farm, Mauchline. Photo: Scottish Tourist Board

Mossgiel as it looked in Burns's time; painting by John Kelso Hunter, mid nineteenth century. Burns Monument and Museum, Kilmarnock

Interior of the kitchen of Mossgiel; wash drawing by William Allan, early nineteenth century. National Gallery of Scotland, Edinburgh, Department of Prints and Drawings. Photo: National Galleries of Scotland

29 Mauchline; watercolour attributed to William Bartlett, *c.* 1840. National Gallery of Scotland, Edinburgh, Department of Prints and Drawings. Photo: National Galleries of Scotland

30–31 *A Poet's Welcome to his Love-begotten Daughter; the First Instance that Entitled him to that Venerable Appellation of Father;* manuscript poem by Robert Burns, 1785. Trustees of the National Library of Scotland, Edinburgh. Ms. 86, ff. 87–88

32 Lovers in a barn; painting by George Morland, 1792. Broderick Castle. Photo: National Trust for Scotland

33 *The Kirk of Scotland's Alarm;* manuscript poem by Robert Burns, 1789. British Museum, Department of Manuscripts. Ms. Eg. 1656, f. 16

34 A Sleepy Congregation. Dr Webster Preaching in Tolbooth Church, Edinburgh; engraving by John Kay. *Kay's Edinburgh Portraits,* 1784–1813

35 Cowgate, Mauchline, showing Jean Armour's house; drawing by John Wilson, 1803. Burns's House Museum, Mauchline

36 Presbyterian Penance; engraving by Tinta after David Allan, 1784. British Museum, Department of Prints and Drawings

37 Last page of a letter from Robert Burns to Mr John Richmond of Cleek, 9 July 1786. Trustees of the National Library of Scotland, Edinburgh. Ms. 98, f. 22

38 Advertisement for the sailing of a *Nancy* on 12 July 1786 from Greenock for Savannah-La-Mer, Jamaica. From *The Glasgow Mercury*, 13–20 July 1786. Mitchell Library, Glasgow

39 *Will ye go to the Indies, my Mary*; manuscript poem by Robert Burns, *c.* 1786. From *The Second Commonplace Book*. Trustees of the Burns Monument, Alloway

41 Proposals, for publishing by subscription, *Scotch Poems*, by Robert Burns. Printed advertisement with the signatures of subscribers, 14 April 1786. Trustees of the Burns Monument, Alloway

Kilmarnock; engraving by J. J. Hinchliffe after William Bartlett. From A. Cunningham: *Pictures and Portraits of the Life and Land of Robert Burns*, 1840. British Museum

Title-page of *Scotch Poems, Chiefly in the Scottish Dialect* by Robert Burns. Kilmarnock, 1786. Trustees of the Burns Monument, Alloway

43 The Gaberlunzie Man, or James V in disguise; watercolour by David Allan, *c.* 1795. Royal Scottish Academy, Edinburgh. Photo: National Galleries of Scotland

44–45 Entry of Prince Charles and the Highlanders into Edinburgh after the Battle of Prestonpans; engraving by Frederick Bacon after Thomas Duncan, after 1840. British Museum

46 Title-page of *Poems* by Robert Fergusson. Edinburgh, 1773. Trustees of the National Library of Scotland, Edinburgh

47 Epitaph for Robert Fergusson; manuscript poem by Robert Burns on the verso of a letter to the Bailies of Canongate Church, Edinburgh, 6 February 1787. Trustees of the Burns Monument, Alloway

48 Page from *Scotticisms Arranged in Alphabetical Order* by James Beattie, 1787

Last page of a letter from Robert Burns to Mr Nicol, 1 June 1787. Trustees of the National Library of Scotland, Edinburgh. Ms. 87, pp. 7–8

50 Poor Mailie; woodcut by Thomas Bewick. From Robert Burns: *Poems*, 1814. British Museum

51 *The Cotter's Saturday Night*; manuscript poem by Robert Burns, 1785. Burns Monument and Museum, Kilmarnock

Holy Bible, 1762, which belonged to William Burnes and was referred to in *The Cotter's Saturday Night*. Trustees of the Burns Monument, Alloway

52 Tam o'Shanter at Alloway Kirk; wash drawing by Alexander Carse, *c.* 1800. National Gallery of Scotland, Edinburgh, Department of Prints and Drawings. Photo: National Galleries of Scotland

53 Preface to *Poems, Chiefly in the Scottish Dialect* by Robert Burns, Edinburgh, 1787. Trustees of the National Library of Scotland, Edinburgh

54 Opening paragraph of a review of *Poems, Chiefly in the Scottish Dialect*; from *The Monthly Review*, December 1786. Mitchell Library, Glasgow

55 Henry Mackenzie; painting by Colvin Smith, *c.* 1820. Scottish National Portrait Gallery, Edinburgh. Photo: National Galleries of Scotland

56 Edinburgh from St Anthony's Chapel; pen and wash drawing by Alexander Carse, 1799. National Gallery of Scotland, Edinburgh, Department of Prints and Drawings. Photo: National Galleries of Scotland

57 Baxter's Close, Edinburgh; watercolour by Henry Duguid, mid nineteenth century. National Gallery of Scotland, Edinburgh, Department of Prints and Drawings. Photo: National Galleries of Scotland

58 George Square; anonymous watercolour. National Gallery of Scotland, Edinburgh, Department of Prints and Drawings. Photo: National Galleries of Scotland

59 Letter from Robert Burns to Gavin Hamilton, 7 December 1786. Haverford College Library, Quaker Collection

60 James, Earl of Glencairn; anonymous miniature, late eighteenth century. Private collection. Photo: National Galleries of Scotland

61 Professor Dugald Stewart with his wife and child; painting by Alexander Nasmyth, c. 1780. Courtesy Ronald Watson, Esq. Photo: National Galleries of Scotland

62 Lord Monboddo; engraving by John Kay, 1799. From *Kay's Edinburgh Portraits*, 1784–1813

Elizabeth Burnett. From *Catalogue of the Burns Exhibition*, 1896. Scottish National Portrait Gallery, Edinburgh. Photo: National Galleries of Scotland

63 Party at Lord Monboddo's house; watercolour by J. Edgar, early nineteenth century. Scottish National Portrait Gallery, Edinburgh. Photo: National Galleries of Scotland

64 Mrs Dunlop; engraving by H. Robinson, c. 1800. Scottish National Portrait Gallery, Edinburgh. Photo: National Galleries of Scotland

65 Walter Scott meeting Robert Burns at Sciennes House; painting by Charles Martin Hardie, 1893. By courtesy of Mrs Maxwell-Scott. Photo: National Galleries of Scotland

66 Smellie's printing office, Anchor Close; watercolour by Henry Duguid, early nineteenth century. National Gallery of Scotland, Edinburgh, Department of Prints and Drawings. Photo: National Galleries of Scotland

67 William Creech; painting by Henry Raeburn, c. 1806. Scottish National Portrait Gallery, Edinburgh. Photo: National Galleries of Scotland

William Smellie; painting by George Watson, after 1792. Scottish National Portrait Gallery, Edinburgh. Photo: National Galleries of Scotland

Stool used by Robert Burns in Smellie's printing office. Lady Stairs Museum, Edinburgh

68 The Old Bridge, Ayr. Photo: Edwin Smith

70 Trial of the first steamboat on Dalswinton Loch, 14 October 1788; engraving. Trustees of the Burns Monument, Alloway

71 Robert Burns; miniature by Alexander Reid, 1795. Scottish National Portrait Gallery, Edinburgh. Photo: National Galleries of Scotland

72 Coldstream Bridge. Photo: Scottish Tourist Board

73 Melrose Abbey. Photo: Edwin Smith

74 Ben Lomond seen from the west across Loch Lomond. Photo: Edwin Smith

75 Jean Armour; watercolour by Samuel Mackenzie, c. 1820. Scottish National Portrait Gallery, Edinburgh. Photo: National Galleries of Scotland

76 Inverness; anonymous watercolour, late eighteenth century. British Museum, Map Room

77 Part of Perth from the north; engraving by James Fittler after John Nattes, 1802. From James Fittler: *Scotia Depicta*, 1804. British Museum

101 Window pane from the Globe Inn, Dumfries, with a verse scratched on by Robert Burns, 1795–96. Trustees of the Burns Monument, Alloway

The Globe Inn, Dumfries. Photo: British Tourist Authority

Design for a stage set for the Dumfries Theatre made at the request of Robert Burns; drawing by Alexander Nasmyth, *c.* 1795. National Gallery of Scotland, Edinburgh, Department of Prints and Drawings. Photo: National Galleries of Scotland

102 Maria Riddell; painting by Thomas Lawrence, *c.* 1800. National Burns Memorial and Cottage Homes, Mauchline

103 The Hermitage, Friar's Carse; anonymous watercolour. National Gallery of Scotland, Edinburgh, Department of Prints and Drawings. Photo: National Galleries of Scotland

104 'Mixtures not always salutary.' A group of men drinking, including Burns; pencil and brown ink drawing by Thomas Stothard, *c.* 1800. Photo: Courtauld Institute of Art

105 Letter from Burns to John M'Murdo, 1792. Trustees of the Burns Monument, Alloway

106 Execution of Louis XVI, 26 January 1793; engraving. Bibliothèque Nationale, Paris. Photo: Françoise Foliot

107 Dr John Moore; painting by Thomas Lawrence, late eighteenth century. Scottish National Portrait Gallery, Edinburgh.

Photo: National Galleries of Scotland

108 An election ballad by Robert Burns for Patrick Heron; manuscript, 1795. Trustees of the Burns Monument, Alloway

109 John Syme; engraving by T. Kelly, *c.* 1800. Scottish National Portrait Gallery, Edinburgh. Photo: National Galleries of Scotland

Letter from Robert Burns to the Lord Provost, Bailies and Town Council of Dumfries, March 1793. British Museum, Department of Manuscripts. Ms.Eg. 1656, f. 7

110 George Thomson; painting by Henry Raeburn, early nineteenth century. From the collection of Viscount Cowdray. Photo: Courtauld Institute of Art

111 Jean Armour Burns with her granddaughter, Sarah; engraving, *c.* 1820. Scottish National Portrait Gallery, Edinburgh. Photo: National Galleries of Scotland

112 The room where Burns died, Dumfries. Photo: Edwin Smith

114 Robert Burns's Monument, Kilmarnock; marble, by W. G. Stevenson, R.S.A. Photo: Scottish Tourist Board

115 Statue of Robert Burns, Irvine; bronze, by Pittendrigh Macgillivray, A.R.S.A. Photo: Scottish Tourist Board

116 Burns and the Muse; sculpture by Hermon Cawthra in the Burns Mausoleum, St Michael's Church, Dumfries. Photo: Scottish Tourist Board

INDEX

The page numbers of illustrations are denoted by italics